COMPREHENSION CLIFFHANGERS

Mysteries

15 Suspenseful Stories That Guide Students to Infer, Visualize, & Summarize to Predict the Ending of Each Story

BILL DOYLE

NEW YORK • TORONTO • LONDON • AUCKLAND • SYDNEY
MEXICO CITY • NEW DELHI • HONG KONG • BUENOS AIRES

Teaching *Resources*

About the Author:

Bill Doyle has written for the Discovery Channel, Random House, Sesame Workshop, Little Brown (including the Crime Through Time mystery series), *TIME for Kids*, and the American Museum of Natural History, among others. Bill invites you to visit him online at www.billdoyle.net.

Editor: Maria L. Chang
Cover design by Brian LaRossa
Interior design by Kathy Massaro
Illustrations by Mike Moran

ISBN-13: 978-0-545-08315-7
ISBN-10: 0-545-08315-X
Copyright © 2010 by Bill Doyle
All rights reserved.
Printed in the U.S.A.

3 4 5 6 7 8 9 10   40   16 15 14 13 12

Contents

Introduction

IT'S NO MYSTERY WHY MYSTERIES CAN MAKE SUCH POWERFUL LEARNING TOOLS. All about discovery and excitement, good mysteries are inherently high-interest tales. They entice readers to keep turning pages until the detective cracks the case and the crook is revealed.

With the fun, action-packed whodunits in this book, we've capitalized on readers' eagerness to solve the case by asking them to stop and reflect just before the climax. The comprehension questions at these points provide learning opportunities that are charged with excitement!

Depending on your students' reading level, you may want to read aloud the first story to illustrate how the stopping points can help enhance their reading experience.

You'll also find a supplemental teacher page accompanying each mystery. The page is broken down into three main sections.

Vocabulary

You may want to review these words and definitions with students before they read the stories.

Before Reading

In this section, you'll find ideas for building background knowledge and how to focus on different reading strategies, such as:

* Making connections
* Understanding genre
* Summarizing
* Making predictions
* Visualizing
* Reading for details
* Understanding literary elements
* Making inferences

After Reading

Discussion ideas and writing prompts offer ways to reinforce skills and foster an enhanced appreciation for reading.

According to *Bringing Words to Life* (Guilford, 2002):

" **Students become interested and enthusiastic about words when instruction is rich and lively.** "

What is more rich and lively than a good mystery?

And Then There Was One...

Before Reading

Background Building

In this mystery, 12-year-old Annie, Pawtown's most famous animal detective, is on the case. This time she must use her sleuthing talent to uncover who is "dog-napping" valuable puppies from the Furry Critters Pet Shop.

To help set the scene, ask students to talk about what kind of animals they would expect to find in a pet shop and let them describe the inside of such a store.

Focus of Reading Strategy: Reading for Details

Picking up details in stories is a valuable skill—especially when reading mysteries. Authors of detective tales will often hide clues in the details, and it can take a careful reader to spot them all.

Point out to students that they should think like detectives when reading this story, keeping an eye out for important details—just as a sleuth looks for clues.

After Reading

Talk About It

Ask students to say the characters' names out loud and to think about them. Elicit that a few of the names help describe the characters, such as Ms. Sellunow (who sells pets in the shop) and Mr. Kees (who works with *keys* as a locksmith).

Discuss why an author might use such a naming technique. Possible conclusions include: these names are more memorable to the reader; they help set a more comical tone.

Write About It

Ask students to pretend that they are Annie, and have them write a short letter to a friend describing this case.

Vocabulary

Here's a list of words your students will come across in this mystery—as well as their definitions:

burly	heavily built
cowered	curled up, showing fear
crocodile tears	fake tears
desperate	in need
detective	a person who works to solve mysteries
forlorn	pitiful, sad
limousine	a large, luxury car
locksmith	a person who makes or fixes locks
sarcastically	not seriously
stammered	had difficulty speaking
suspects	wrongdoers

And Then There Was One . . .

Someone is puppy-napping cute critters, and it's up to Annie to crack the case.

"Nooooo!"

The scream jerked Annie awake. The 12-year-old sat up, banging her head on a puppy cage and sending fur and bits of paper flying.

What the kibble is going on? she wondered, glancing at her watch. It was only 6 A.M. Pawtown's one and only animal detective had been having a nice, peaceful dream about flowing water— and it took her a second to figure out where she was.

On the shelves around her there were cages filled with animals—five red parrots in one, four mutt puppies in another, countless hamsters, ferrets, kittens—even an emu.

Now she remembered. Of course! She was in the Furry Critters Pet Shop. Two days ago, a crook had stolen a valuable bluecoat puppy from the store. Annie had spent last night here, planning to look for clues. But she must have fallen asleep.

"Nooooo!" There was that scream again. With a sinking feeling, Annie jumped to her feet and rushed toward the sound. Two aisles over, she found Ms. Sellunow, the plump woman who ran the pet shop. She was standing next to a large cage, and her face was wet with tears.

"Are you okay?" Annie asked. Before Ms. Sellunow could answer, a tall, thin figure sprinted through the front door. It was Tater, a man who did odd jobs around the shop.

"I was on my way to work and could hear you screaming down the street!" Tater cried, hurrying over to them. "What's happened?"

Ms. Sellunow blew her nose into a blue handkerchief. "I just got here," she sobbed. "A second puppy has been . . . dog-napped!"

She pointed a finger with a gold ring at the cage, which held the small bluecoat dogs—famous for their blue color. Because they were so rare and valuable, Ms. Sellunow had the only key to the cage and only she fed and cared for them.

Annie peered into the cage where the mother dog paced nervously and just one little blue puppy cowered in the corner.

"Another bluecoat is missing?" Tater asked, leaning against the big sink where the animals were bathed. "Those puppies are too young to be without their mom. They could be in danger."

This made Ms. Sellunow sob even louder. She turned to Annie. "When I hired you yesterday to find my stolen puppy, there were still two. Now one more is gone! I thought you were supposed to be a great animal detective."

Annie said miserably, "I am." Or at least she wanted to be. Right now she felt like a failure. How could she have fallen asleep on the job?

Just then, a burly man wearing a fancy black suit burst into the store and stormed over to them. Annie recognized Mr. Kees right away. He owned three stores in town that sold keys and locks.

"I must have a blue puppy today, Ms. Sellunow!" he demanded. "The mayor is coming over to my house, and I need to have the best dog. I'll pay any price."

Ms. Sellunow stepped between him and the bluecoats' cage. "I've told you again and again, Mr. Kees, I've already sold these puppies to Mrs. Gotrocks. When they're old enough to leave their mother, she'll get them. And no one else."

Turning so red that he looked like a balloon about to pop, Mr. Kees shouted, "I'll get one of those blue dogs. Just you wait!" He left the shop, slamming the door and speeding away in his limousine.

Ms. Sellunow was still crying. "I don't care about money," she moaned. "I'd never sell my puppies to a person like Mr. Kees."

Not sure what to do now, Annie ran a hand through her hair—and her fingers touched something. She plucked free a piece of paper about half the size of an index card. "What's this?" she wondered out loud.

Ms. Sellunow sniffled. "A clue it's time to wash your hair?" She didn't wait for an answer. "I'm going in the back to weep for my lost bluecoats." With her silver bracelets jangling, Ms. Sellunow wandered off to the back of the shop.

Annie looked down at the paper in her hand. It had yesterday's date and read:

Three Mutt Puppies for Sale! Get Them CHEAP! She never understood why mutts were sold for so much less than purebred dogs like the bluecoats. Mutts were just as good as pets.

The little sign must have fallen into her hair when she banged her head against the mutts' cage. Annie's instincts told her it might be an important clue, but she couldn't figure out how it would help crack the case.

If only Annie could think. But a loud crunching sound kept distracting her. Tater was standing next to her, eating dog biscuits that were shaped like little bones.

"I brought a sandwich with me last night," Annie said, feeling sorry for him. "Do you want half?"

"No, thanks," Tater said through a mouthful of biscuits. "I like this stuff."

Annie didn't think that was possible. She had once been trapped in the wilderness for two weeks, and she wasn't sure she'd have eaten dog treats even then.

"Maybe you should make sure Ms. Sellunow is okay," Annie suggested. Tater nodded and slinked off, still munching away.

Alone now, Annie thought about the case and the main suspects. Who could be stealing the bluecoat puppies? Ms. Sellunow had the only key to the cage, but Mr. Kees was a locksmith. Did he pick the lock on the cage and steal the puppies? And then there was Tater. Was he eating dog treats because he was desperate for money—desperate enough to nab the puppies and sell them to Mr. Kees?

Annie turned her attention back to the cage. The bluecoat mother was pacing in there, looking forlorn. If only she could tell Annie what had happened to her puppies.

Maybe she can, Annie thought, spotting something in the dog's mouth. Annie smooshed her face up against the cage to get a better look. It was a piece of blue cloth.

That's when all the clues came together. The sound of flowing water in her dream, the piece of cloth, the sign about the mutts...everything clicked into place!

Annie let out a howl of excitement, thinking she might have solved the case. To make sure, though, she would wait until tonight to spring her trap.

Ten hours later, the shop was closed for business. The lights were off, and most of the animals were asleep in the darkness. Annie was lying on the floor, pretending to snore.

She could hear the sound of the front door opening and closing. The dog-napper was in the shop. Footsteps headed slowly toward the cage holding the last bluecoat puppy.

In the blink of an eye, Annie sat up and clicked on her flashlight, trapping the crook in the beam of light. "Hello," Annie said. "I've been expecting you."

Comprehension Cliffhangers: Mysteries © 2010 by Bill Doyle, Scholastic Inc.

Stop Here!

Discussion Questions

1. How many puppies have been dog-napped? What makes them so special?

2. Can you name the three main suspects? What reason might each one have to take the puppies?

3. Which character do you think Annie is speaking to when she says, "I've been expecting you"? Who do you think the crook is?

4. Talk about possible ways this story could end. Can you predict what will happen?

OKAY! **Now keep reading to see if you were right.**

Getting to her feet, Annie kept the flashlight pointed at the shopkeeper. "Good evening, Ms. Sellunow."

Looking surprised, Ms. Sellunow froze next to the bluecoats' cage. She stammered, "I just came here…"

"To steal another animal?" Annie finished for her.

"You think I'm the bad guy?" Ms. Sellunow started sobbing—again. "Why would I steal my own bluecoat puppies?"

"Because you never had them," Annie said, not buying the woman's crocodile tears.

The plump woman pretended to be shocked. "You saw them with your own eyes! Look, there's one now!" Ms. Sellunow pointed at the blue fur ball in the cage.

Annie shook her head. "That isn't a bluecoat. It's a mutt. You used blue dye to make the mutts look like bluecoats. Then you sold the fake puppies to make some quick money."

"Money?" Ms. Sellunow cried. "I don't care about money!"

"You say that, but you're covered in gold and silver jewelry," Annie said, gesturing to the woman's rings and bracelets. Ms. Sellunow didn't bother arguing.

"You knew that if the puppies went home with Mrs. Gotrocks, she would learn the truth," Annie continued. "But you wouldn't have to give the money back if the puppies were stolen first. So you hired me to make your dog-napping story more believable."

"But you know the real story, do you?" the woman said, rubbing her eyes.

"That's right," Annie said. "The past two nights you came in here and took one of the phony puppies out of the bluecoats' cage and washed off the blue dye." Annie flashed her light on the sink used to bathe the animals and then back on Ms. Sellunow. "That's why I dreamt about running water—I heard the sound from the faucet even though I was asleep."

"I think you're still dreaming, dear," Ms. Sellunow said sarcastically. "I don't have to listen to this."

Before she could walk away, Annie stopped her. "There's more. At some point, the bluecoat female bit off a piece of the handkerchief you used to dry the mutt. I found the cloth in her mouth, and I'd bet it would perfectly match your handkerchief."

Mrs. Sellunow threw up her hands in disbelief. "And where did I stash this squeaky-clean mutt?"

"In with the other mutts, of course," Annie answered. "This morning I noticed there were four mutts in that cage. But according to this sign, there should only be three." Annie held up the paper that read: *Three Mutt Puppies for Sale! Get Them CHEAP!* "The extra mutt is the one you washed off and put in with the others last night."

Suddenly, all the fake sadness drained out of Ms. Sellunow's face. She looked like an angry, cornered animal ready to pounce. "So what if you're right?" she hissed. "No one is going to believe *you*."

"I wouldn't be too sure about that," Annie said.

That was when Tater stepped out of the shadows where Annie had asked him to watch and listen. "I believe Annie," he told Ms. Sellunow. "We're going to call the police, and you're going to give back Mrs. Gotrocks' money."

Ms. Sellunow seemed to realize she was caught. "Oh, no," she whined, and slumped against the wall. She started sobbing, and for the first time Annie thought there were real tears.

"Are you going to lose your job?" Annie asked Tater, worried about his future.

Tater smiled. "Actually, this is my store. Ms. Sellunow just worked here. And, guess what, Ms. Sellunow?' he asked, popping a dog biscuit into his mouth. "You're fired."

Comprehension Cliffhangers: Mysteries © 2010 by Bill Doyle, Scholastic Inc.

Something Fishy in the Forest

Before Reading

Background Building

Readers hit the trail with animal detective Annie and her best friend, Cindy, in this mystery. To help set the scene and context of the action, ask students if they have ever been hiking. What can hikers expect to see on a mountain trail or in the woods? What should they be cautious of? Can trails be treacherous? Ask students about the clothes hikers might wear and what they might eat.

Focus of Reading Strategy: Understanding Literary Elements—Setting

Explain to students that the setting is the place and time in which a story takes place. Point out that setting can determine what action takes place and how characters behave. Ask students to identify the setting of this story.

After Reading

Talk About It

Annie, the detective hero in this story, specializes in cracking cases that deal with animals. Ask students to brainstorm other types of interesting detectives, such as an art detective or a food detective. Discuss what kinds of cases these detectives might work on.

Write About It

This story is not completely linear; it does not go straight from one point in time to a later point in chronological order. (There is a flashback just after the start of the story.) Have students create a linear timeline of events starting with Annie and Cindy hitting the trail and ending with them discovering the identity of their pursuer.

Vocabulary

Here's a list of words your students will come across in this mystery—as well as their definitions:

crouched	squatted close to the ground
dangled	hung freely
determined	having one's mind made up
embarrassed	feeling shame or wounded pride
fiftieth	position 50 in a series of things
footing	a position of stability
plunged	dropped into
prickly	covered with protective thorns, spines, or barbs
pursuer	a person or thing trying to overtake or capture another
shadowy	filled with shade
trailhead	the beginning of a trail

Something Fishy in the Forest

Are Annie and her best friend being followed down a dangerous trail?

"Achoo!" Twelve-year-old Cindy suddenly sneezed, and her foot slipped off the narrow hiking trail. For one terrifying second, Cindy dangled over the edge of the cliff and the 50-foot drop to the rocky riverbed below. Then Annie's hand shot out, grabbed Cindy's backpack, and pulled her best friend back to safety.

Leaning against a huge boulder, the two girls caught their breath. Their hearts were racing.

"Whoa," Annie finally said. "That was close. Are you okay?"

Cindy was still shaking from the fright, but she nodded. "I guess that sneeze made me slip. I only sneeze around people's pets. And when I get nervous. Like now!"

Annie couldn't blame Cindy for being freaked out. For the past five hours, the two girls had been hiking in the woods of Mount Pawtown. When they had started out that morning with their backpacks full of snacks and water, the spring sun had been shining brightly. They had climbed to the lake at the top of the mountain, telling each other jokes and checking out the wildlife. It had been fun.

Then everything changed.

As they were heading back down the mountain, storm clouds had begun gathering overhead. Even worse, they had started hearing strange noises in the woods. The noises seemed to be coming from right behind them and sounded like: *Thwatttchhhhh. Thwatttchhhh.*

"What in the kibble is going on?" Annie wondered again for the fiftieth time.

"Is someone—or something—following us?" Cindy asked now, pushing away from the boulder and looking back along the trail.

"I don't know," Annie said. Normally, she would have had an answer. After all, she was Pawtown's one and only animal detective and an expert at solving outdoor cases. But she had never heard such a strange sound like this in the wilderness before.

Annie smiled, trying to make Cindy feel better. "Whatever was making that noise is probably way behind us by now—"

Thwatttchhhhh.

Annie was interrupted by the noise. It came from the shadowy trees about 20 feet behind them.

Determined to solve the mystery, Annie walked back to investigate. But she couldn't spot anything in the prickly bushes that lined the trail or between the thick trunks of the trees. Whatever was making the creepy noise was hidden in the forest.

"What *is* it?" Cindy whispered to Annie when she returned.

Annie could only guess. "Maybe some kind of animal like..." She trailed off.

"Like what?" Cindy insisted.

Annie had been about to say, "...like a bear." But she had stopped herself. She didn't want to make Cindy any more scared than she was.

"Nothing, don't worry," Annie said. She looked at her watch and glanced up at the cloudy sky. "We better keep going. It's still two miles to the trailhead. We don't want to get stuck out here in the dark."

"You got that right," Cindy agreed. She looked around with wide eyes and then sneezed again.

The girls headed down the mountain. In about a half mile, the trail led them to a stream. Without stopping, Cindy started to wade through the icy water to get to the other side.

"No, wait," Annie said. "Remember, the water in the middle is too deep. We have to cross like we did before." She pointed to a log that been placed across the stream as a kind of bridge.

"Oh, right," Cindy said. "I guess I'm so ready to get off the mountain, I forgot." Stepping up on the log, she put her hands out like a tightrope walker and quickly crossed the stream. "Come on, Annie, hurry!" she called from the other side.

Just as Annie was crossing the log, she heard the sound behind her. *Thwatchhhh.*

Annie turned her head fast to try to catch a glimpse of their pursuer. She couldn't see anything—and her quick movements made her nearly lose her balance. For a scary moment, she almost plunged into the stream.

"Annie!" Cindy cried. "Watch where you're going!"

Annie got her footing back and continued across to where Cindy was waiting for her. Immediately, Annie crouched down and started pulling on the log. It was too heavy for her to move by herself.

"Help me, Cindy," Annie said. Cindy grabbed onto the log, and together they were able to pull it through the water to their side of the stream.

"There," Annie said, satisfied. "We've gotten rid of the log bridge."

"Good job!" Cindy said happily. "The only way anything could follow us now would be to climb up that tree on the other side and leap across the stream. No one could do that!"

The girls gave each other high fives and headed down the trail again.

Thirty minutes later, after walking another mile, they took a break. Sitting with their backs up against a wooden post, they munched on their last two apples.

At the top of the post was a sign with an arrow pointing down the mountain and the words:

CAMP COMFORT 1 MILE

Annie thought of Camp Comfort. It was a big, friendly place with cabins and a mess hall. The owners of the camp had three dogs who loved to fetch and a big, friendly cat named Snowball who curled up next to the laundry line. Snowball sometimes hid in campers' sleeping bags. Annie couldn't wait to get to the camp, have a cold soda, and curl up in her own sleeping bag.

As they finished their apples, the wind changed direction, and Cindy's nose wrinkled. "Yuck!" she said. "What's that smell?"

Annie's nose picked it up, too, and she grinned. "I can solve that mystery at least." Annie reached over and plucked something slimy and scaly off the back of Cindy's hiking boot. "You must have stepped on a fish tail up at the lake." Annie tossed it into the woods.

"Yuck!" Cindy squealed, and for some reason her reaction made them both laugh. It really wasn't that funny, but it felt good to forget about possibly being followed. Just then—

Comprehension Cliffhangers: Mysteries © 2010 by Bill Doyle, Scholastic Inc.

Thwattchhhh.

The sound in the woods had returned.

Whatever was making the noise had managed to get across the stream even without the log bridge. And it was still following them! Cindy's eyes went wide, and she looked ready to jump up and run.

"Wait!" said Annie, holding out a hand to stop her. "Don't panic! I'll be right back."

"Where are you going?" Cindy asked in a frightened voice, then sneezed.

"This has gone far enough," Annie said. "I'm going solve this case and find out what's following us."

Leaving Cindy sitting against the post, Annie crept quietly back along the trail and into the woods. She didn't see any tracks. Just a wide mark on the ground as if something had been dragged in the dirt. Then Annie spotted a foot-long piece of white cord dangling from a low bush.

Suddenly, Annie let out a howl of excitement as all the clues clicked into place. And just in time.

From the other side of the trees, she could hear Cindy shout, "Something's coming!"

Annie didn't panic. Instead, the animal detective smiled.

Thanks to all the clues, she knew exactly what was happening.

Discussion Questions

1. What two things can make Cindy sneeze?

2. Why did Annie and Cindy pull the log to one side of the stream? How did the girls think this would help their situation?

3. When Annie heard Cindy shout, why do you think Annie smiled? Can you name which clues she is thinking about?

4. What (or who) do you think is following the girls?

 Now keep reading to see if your predictions were right!

Smiling, Annie walked back through the group of trees to her friend. There she was, still sitting on the grassy ground under the signpost. Only now she was petting a fluffy white cat that was curled up on her lap and purring like crazy.

Crouching down so she could pet the cat, too, Annie said, "I see you've met Snowball!"

Cindy read the tag on the cat's collar. "It says, 'My name is Snowball.' How did you know, Annie?"

"All the clues pointed right at it," Annie said. "For one thing, you only sneeze when you get nervous and when you're around pets...like cats! And some cats are great tree climbers."

Cindy's eyes lit up. "That's how it was able to cross the stream even after we moved the log bridge!" After a second, she frowned and asked, "But why was Snowball following us to begin with? How did a cat get all the way out here in the wilderness?"

Ready with the answer, Annie said, "Snowball loves to curl up in campers' sleeping bags. I bet she fell asleep in one and was taken accidentally to the top of the mountain. Then, when she smelled the fish tail stuck to your shoe, she started following us. The poor thing just wanted to go home, but she was scared to get too close to us."

"Okay," Cindy nodded. "That all makes sense. But what about that creepy noise we kept hearing?"

Annie showed her the short piece of white cord she found dangling on the branch. "This is part of a laundry line. It must have gotten stuck on Snowball's collar down at Camp Comfort. She's been dragging it behind her along the ground, and it was making strange noises."

Grinning, Annie waited for Cindy to congratulate her on her powers of detection. Instead, her friend sneezed.

Annie laughed. "You better give me Snowball before you sneeze your head off."

Cindy shook her head. "It isn't Snowball. I'm sneezing because I'm nervous."

"You're nervous?" Annie asked, surprised. "About what?"

Looking down at the now sleeping cat in her lap, Cindy gave a little embarrassed smile. "About telling people how scared I was being chased by Snowball—the world's friendliest cat!"

Creature Features

The Parrot Whodunit

Before Reading

Background Building

Tell students that *whodunit* is another way of saying *mystery*. Write the word on the board and ask why it's a good name. Elicit the response that it sums up the heart of most mysteries, which is "who done it?" Ask if students can think of other colorful words or phrases used when talking about mysteries. Possible answers include *case cracker*, *private eye*, *gumshoe*, and *secret agent*.

Focus of Reading Strategy: Summarizing

A summary is a shortened version of something, and it usually covers only important points. Good readers are able to recall and retell major events from a story and condense them into a short summary. Ask students to think about major points they might include in a summary while reading this story.

After Reading

Talk About It

Suggest that students can think of clues as bricks. In order to crack the case, a good detective will stack up clues and see how they stand. If the clues are strong and have been stacked correctly, they might form a solid solution.

Ask students to list clues they discover in "The Parrot Whodunit." What clues does Annie "stack up" to uncover the identity of the crook?

Write About It

Challenge students to write a summary of this story in five sentences or less. Have volunteers read their sentences out loud. After each reading, ask the class if the summary covers all the main points of the story.

Now ask students to summarize a favorite book—either one they have read on their own or as part of class work—in five sentences or less.

Vocabulary

Here's a list of words your students will come across in this mystery—as well as their definitions:

crooked	irregular in shape; not straight
evidence	facts and information used to prove a point
flourish	showy gesture
fluttered	flapped up and down
gloomily	with an air of depression
gobbling	eating hastily
landmarks	buildings or sites with historical significance
miserably	unhappily
papier-mâché	material made from paper pulp that can be shaped and painted
patience	ability to deal with problems without getting upset
pyramidal	resembling a pyramid
slumped	sank heavily
suspended	hung from

The Parrot Whodunit

When a bird confesses to a crime, Annie cries *fowl!*

"Hi, Annie," Sam said, opening the front door and letting Pawtown's one and only animal detective into his apartment. "Thanks for coming over so fast."

"No problem," Annie said, sweating a little from rushing over on this hot Sunday afternoon. "You sounded really freaked out when you called and said it was an emergency. Where are your parents?"

"Out for the day," he said, as Annie followed him into the living room. "They left me to watch over my twin brothers. This is something only you can help me with, anyway."

Annie nearly howled in excitement. Could this be the beginning of an animal mystery? There was nothing she liked more than sinking her teeth into a good case. "What's up?" she asked, trying to contain herself.

"Not my grades, that's for sure," Sam said gloomily. "I called you because something horrible has happened to my history project."

Sam and Annie were both in the sixth grade at Pawtown Middle School. Their history teacher, Mr. Noitall, had asked them to build models of famous landmarks, and the projects were due tomorrow.

"What did you make?" Annie asked. She had just finished building a copy of the White House out of papier-mâché. It was a little crooked, but she was proud of it.

"I constructed one of the ancient pyramids," Sam said. Then he added, "Out of chocolate."

"What the kibble did you say?" Annie thought maybe she didn't hear him correctly. "You built a pyramidal landmark out of chocolate?" she asked. "Why would you do something like that? That sounds like the real mystery."

"Okay, I guess it wasn't the best idea for building material," he said miserably. "But that's not why I called you." Sam took a breath and said, "Someone ate my pyramid."

"Aha!" exclaimed Annie. "And you want me to help you figure out who did it?"

"No," Sam said. "I know who did it. I just want you to help me figure out what to do with the crook."

"I don't get it," Annie said, both disappointed and confused.

"Follow me," Sam instructed. He led her down a short hallway toward his room. On the way, they passed another bedroom. Sam's 9-year-old twin brothers, Nate and Marvin, were sitting on the floor inside, eating crackers out of a box and playing a video game. A small fort made out of sheets and two chairs was in one corner of their messy room.

Giving Nate and Marvin a wave, Annie said, "Hey, guys."

"Hi!" Nate chirped with a friendly smile.

The other twin, Marvin, didn't speak and seemed distracted by the game.

Annie was used to hanging around animals, but she couldn't stand it when people were rude. "What's the deal with Marvin?" she asked Sam. "I've met monkeys with more manners."

Sam stopped outside his room and explained, "Marvin's got a sore throat and can barely talk. Nate is a good brother, though. He asked me to run down to the laundry room in the basement to grab a blanket this morning. He added it to the fort he built to make Marvin feel better. I guess Nate forgot that Marvin is scared of small spaces and never goes inside forts."

"Hmmm," Annie said. It was interesting, but she was eager to get back to the case. "Show me the scene of the crime."

Sam opened the door. There was a wooden base about the size of a microwave oven on the floor near the bed. In one corner of the room, a birdcage was suspended from the ceiling. Inside was a beautiful green and red parrot.

Comprehension Cliffhangers: Mysteries © 2010 by Bill Doyle, Scholastic Inc.

"Wow!" Annie gushed at the sight of the bird. She had never seen such a gorgeous parrot.

"That's Jenkins," Sam said bitterly. "That bird ruined my history grade."

Keeping her eyes on Jenkins, Annie said, "Tell me what happened."

Sam slumped onto his bed to tell his story. "After I went down to the laundry room earlier, I came back in here and saw that my pyramid was missing from its spot." He pointed at the bare wooden base where there were just a few chocolate crumbs. "Jenkins was in his cage, but the cage door was open. I said, 'Who did this? Who took my pyramid?' out loud, not really thinking I'd get an answer. And then Jenkins said..."

As if on cue, Jenkins tilted his head and said in a high-pitched voice, "I did it, I did it, I did it." Then the bird fluttered his clipped wings as if he was proud of himself.

"Did you hear that, Annie?" Sam demanded. "That's what he said before. Jenkins confessed to eating the pyramid! He must have done it when I went to the laundry room."

Before Annie could answer, the parrot repeated, "I did it, I did it, I did it."

As Jenkins spoke, he rocked back and forth on his perch in excitement. Annie stepped even closer to the cage. The latch on the cage door was flimsy. It could have been opened by a smart bird. And he might have gotten out of the cage for a bit. But how could a small bird like Jenkins eat so much chocolate in such a short amount of time?

Thinking for a second, Annie looked at Sam. "Was anyone else in the apartment this morning?"

Shaking his head, Sam said, "No, just me and my twin brothers."

"Huh," Annie said. She turned back to study the bird again. This time she noticed something stuck in his feathers. She carefully put two fingers between the bars of the cage and plucked the crumb free. "What's this?"

Getting up to take a look at the small piece of food, Sam said, "Must be chocolate."

Annie sniffed the crumb. "It's not chocolate. It looks and smells more like a cracker."

"It can't be," Sam said. "I haven't given Jenkins a cracker today. He only gets one when he does something good. Like when he sings or repeats something I've said. A cracker is a reward." Sam sat down heavily on his bed again, discouraged. "So what am I going to do with this bird?"

Annie shrugged. "You could start by apologizing."

Raising his eyebrows in surprise, Sam asked, "What do you mean?"

"Tell Jenkins you're sorry for falsely accusing him. This bit of cracker has just helped me crack this case! I know who took your pyramid, and poor Jenkins didn't have anything to do with it!"

Comprehension Cliffhangers: Mysteries © 2010 by Bill Doyle, Scholastic Inc.

 **Discussion Questions**

1. Why is Sam so upset when Annie arrives at the apartment?

2. Who does Sam think took his school project? How does he think it happened? What proof does he have?

3. Who else is in the apartment? Is one of those two boys sick? What's wrong with him?

4. Does Annie agree with Sam and his pick of the crook? Who do you think Annie believes is the bad guy? Why?

 Now keep reading to see if your predictions were correct.

"Come on," Annie said, leading the way out of Sam's room and back down the hall. She barged into the twins' room, where they were still playing video games and gobbling snacks out of the box.

"We're busy," Marvin rasped.

Annie had no more patience for rudeness and snapped off the TV.

"Hey!" Marvin tried to shout, but his sore throat prevented him from making more than a squeak. Standing in front of the dark TV screen, Annie put her hands on her hips. "I need to talk to you two, Nate and Marvin, and I want your attention."

"What's going on, Annie?" Sam asked.

"One of your brothers took your pyramid, Sam," she announced.

"What?" croaked Marvin.

"But that's silly!" Sam said. "Jenkins said he did it."

Annie shook her head. "Parrots don't come up with words by themselves. They only repeat things they've heard. Someone gave Jenkins a cracker to train him to say 'I did it' over and over. That's why we found the piece of cracker in his feathers."

Sam thought about this for a second. "Okay," he said. "But which twin?"

"Marvin has a sore throat," Annie answered. "He can barely talk, and he couldn't train Jenkins to say anything." She paused dramatically and then pointed a finger at Nate. "So the real crook must be Nate. He must have taken the

chocolate pyramid when he sent you downstairs to get the blanket for the fort."

"No way!" Nate protested, shoving the snack box out of sight.

Rushing across the room, Sam grabbed the box. "This is a box of crackers! It was you, Nate!"

"I didn't do it!" Nate shouted. "I wouldn't have had time to eat it all. And where would I hide something that big?"

Annie had an answer for that, too. "Somewhere you knew your twin brother, who is afraid of small spaces, wouldn't go."

Before Sam could ask what she meant, Annie strode across the room to the fort that Nate had built out of blankets and two chairs. With a flourish, she pulled back the top blanket as if she were revealing a sculpture at an art show. On the floor between the two chairs was Sam's foot-high chocolate pyramid. It was still in pretty good shape. There was just one small bite mark on the top. Sam could easily fix that and would be able to bring it to school the next day.

"Do you want to change your tune, Nate?" Annie asked, wheeling on the now-speechless twin.

Seeing all the evidence piled up against him, Nate finally cracked. "I love chocolate so much, I couldn't resist! I'm sorry, Sam!"

Nate looked ready to cry, and Annie had to admit he did look genuinely sorry. For a moment, Sam didn't say anything. Then, with a forgiving smile, he tousled Nate's hair and said, "It's okay. At least now I know who the real birdbrain in the family is!"

Loot Lookers

Mugged by a Martian

Before Reading

Background Building

Many mysteries, such as this one, take place in a secluded mansion on a dark and stormy night. Have students imagine what such a setting might look like, and ask them to share their ideas with the class.

Discuss with students why this setting is used by so many authors. Possible reasons might include...

- ❊ **Isolation:** With authorities or police far away, the danger and excitement are heightened.
- ❊ **Mood:** The storm creates an added element of spookiness.
- ❊ **Central location:** Putting all the characters in one place, such as a mansion, makes it easier to keep the action moving ahead quickly.

Focus of Reading Strategy:
Asking Questions

Like a clever detective on a case, a good reader asks questions while reading a story. Questions can lead to a better understanding of the text. Have your students write down questions they might have as they read this mystery.

After Reading

Talk About It

Ask students to share some of the questions they wrote down while reading the story. Were they able to answer their own questions by the end of the mystery? If not, open up the questions to the class.

Write About It

Have students create an invitation to the costume ball described in this story. They should include facts they picked up in their reading, such as location, theme of the ball, and host. Students can also enhance the invitations with extra details and drawings.

Vocabulary

Here's a list of words your students will come across in this mystery—as well as their definitions:

aardvark	burrowing animal with a long snout that eats termites
agency	company or organization
assured	convinced a person of something
complicated	difficult to understand
condescending	behaving in a way that shows one thinks he or she is superior to others
detained	kept in custody
grimace	expression that shows discomfort
mansion	a large house
Martian	a creature from Mars
overwrought	upset or emotional
reception hall	area where guests are greeted and possibly entertained
sculpted	carved

Mugged by a Martian

When an alien nabs a necklace, it's up to Natalie and Harry to bring the case down to Earth.

A year ago, Natalie and Harry started their own detective agency, called the Loot Lookers. People hired the 12-year-old friends to track down missing items or stolen treasure. And that was exactly what they were doing in the Henderson mansion on this dark and stormy night.

Their pal from school, a huge football player named Alex Henderson, had called and asked them to come out to his great-grandmother's estate. There had been a costume ball in the reception hall that night. During the last dance, a diamond necklace had been stolen right off Mrs. Henderson's neck.

"Can you tell us what happened?" Harry asked after Alex had led them into the reception hall and introduced them to his great-grandmother.

"A Martian stole my diamond necklace, that's what happened!" Mrs. Henderson cried. Then she noticed how distracted Natalie seemed by all of the expensive things in the room, including an aardvark sculpted out of gold. "Are you listening to me, young lady?" the elderly woman demanded, looking ready to whack Natalie with her cane.

Harry took a step between them, holding up his hands. "We're listening, Mrs. Henderson," he assured her. "Tell us what happened."

"Very well," Mrs. Henderson sighed, touching her neck where the strand of diamonds used to be. "Sorry if I seem a little overwrought. That necklace has been in my family for generations. I know it seems like I have it all. But that necklace is the only material thing that means something to me."

"Why do you think a Martian stole it?" Harry asked. He tried not to sound condescending, but he couldn't help it.

"Not an actual Martian, dear," Mrs. Henderson said, rolling her eyes. "I'm not completely kooky. We were hosting the Space Association costume ball here tonight." She pointed one bony finger to the corner of the room. "I was over there watching everyone dancing through my telescope."

"A telescope?" Natalie asked. This strange piece of information finally got her attention, and she wandered over to look at the telescope that sat atop a large, black tripod. "You use this to look at people in the same room as you?"

Their friend Alex chuckled. "Granny doesn't like to use eyeglasses. So she sits in the corner during parties and watches people through a telescope."

Nodding as if there were nothing odd about that, Mrs. Henderson said, "That's right. But tonight it was strange. Everything in the telescope was in black and white. Something must be wrong with it."

Natalie peered through the lens and then ran a hand along the telescope. "It's working fine now," she said, and then made a face. "Hold on. There's something sticky on the other end here. It feels almost like glue."

Harry's ears perked up at this information, but Mrs. Henderson wasn't listening. She continued, "I saw someone dressed as a Martian, with four antennae, coming across the room toward me. Then my necklace was gone!"

Clapping her hands in satisfaction, Natalie said, "Well, that's easy. Whoever was dressed as a Martian is your crook."

With a grimace, Alex shook his head. "It's more complicated than that. The theme of the ball this year was Mars. So everyone was wearing Martian costumes tonight. Any one of the guests could have taken the necklace."

"That means all the guest are suspects," Harry said. "Where are they?"

Mrs. Henderson pointed to a door. "I've had them detained in the library. They all emptied their pockets. There are keys, cell phones, digital media players, wallets—but no necklace."

"Come on, Natalie and Harry, you can talk to them," Alex said. "The guests agreed to speak to you instead of the police. No one wants trouble. But they are all anxious to leave."

Alex opened a door and showed the Loot Lookers into the library. Inside, the 15 suspects from the party looked so strange! Lined up in front of a bookshelf, each wore a Martian costume, but in a slightly different way. Some had two or three antennae, others had four or five. Some wore sparkly glitter or had fake eyes or extra limbs.

But they all shared one thing. They were angry.

"You can't keep us here!" shouted a Martian with three antennae. "I agreed to stay for a while, but now I'm tired and I want to leave at once!" There were cranky rumbles of agreement from the others.

"Okay," Harry said reasonably. "Everyone with four antennae on their heads can go right now."

There were cries of relief from six Martians with four antennae as they headed for the door.

"Wait!" Natalie shouted and held up her hands to stop them. She turned to her partner. "Harry, why are you letting the prime suspects go? Mrs. Henderson said the crook had four antennae. That's our only clue!"

"Not our only one, Natalie. You found one yourself."

She dropped her hands, confused. "I did?"

Harry didn't answer. Instead, he signaled for the Martians with four antennae to leave. "The rest of you can go, too," he told the nine remaining suspects. "But first, I want to ask you a question. Which of you have a portable digital media player?"

Five Martians raised their hands.

"Okay," Harry said. "If you didn't raise your hand, you can leave."

Natalie wanted to clobber her partner. "What are you doing, Harry? This makes no sense!"

Holding up a finger to tell her to be patient, Harry said to the five remaining Martians, "Finally, before the rest of you go, I would just like to shake everyone's hand. In fact, I would like my partner Natalie to do it."

Natalie was about to protest, but realized it would be pointless. When Harry got a plan in his head, it was hard to convince him to drop it. She shrugged and started shaking the five remaining Martians' hands. When she shook the hand of the third one, a Martian with three antennae and an extra eye on his costume, she stopped.

Natalie looked at her hand and then up at Harry. She was smiling. Now she got it!

"Okay, everyone else can leave. Everyone except you," Natalie announced and pointed a finger at the Martian with the extra eye.

Comprehension Cliffhangers: Mysteries © 2010 by Bill Doyle, Scholastic Inc.

Discussion Questions

1. Who are the Loot Lookers? What do they do?

2. What has been stolen from Mrs. Henderson? Does she know who took it?

3. What kind of party took place at the mansion before Natalie and Harry arrived? Why does the party make it harder to figure out the identity of the crook?

4. Can you guess why Harry let the Martians with four antennae leave the room? Think of a few good reasons.

OKAY! **Now keep reading to see if you cracked the case!**

Minutes later, Mrs. Henderson was in the library clutching her diamond necklace with tears of gratitude streaming down her cheeks. The Loot Lookers had found the necklace hidden beneath the costume of the Martian with the extra eye.

"How did you two know the crook was this guy?" Alex asked Natalie and Harry. Alex was sitting on the bad guy, using his immense weight to pin the Martian to the floor until the police arrived.

Harry said, "The first clue came when Mrs. Henderson said she saw things in black and white through the telescope."

"Why was that a clue?" Mrs. Henderson asked.

"There are a lot of old black-and-white science fiction movies with Martians," Harry said. "I figured the crook downloaded one and stuck his digital player onto the end of the telescope with an adhesive. That way, when Mrs. Henderson looked through the lens, she saw the movie—not what was actually happening. While she watched the movie, the crook grabbed the necklace. Then he removed his digital player and disappeared back into the crowd."

"But he left glue behind," Natalie explained. "That's why the telescope was sticky when I touched it earlier—and why his hand was sticky when I shook it a few minutes ago. I knew he was the bad guy because he had glue on his hand!"

"Wow," Alex said, impressed by their detective work. "But, Harry, why did

27

you let everyone with four antennae go right away?"

"The crook picked a movie with a Martian with four antennae," Harry responded. "He knew we would look for someone who matched that description. I decided he would try to throw us off his trail by having a different number of antennae on his own costume. So—"

"So everyone with four antennae would be innocent!" Alex said, finishing Harry's sentence. In his excitement, Alex shifted his weight, prompting a groan from the Martian underneath him.

"You promised I could leave!" the Martian complained.

Just then, Harry heard the police coming through the front door. "You're right, and I never break a promise," Harry said to the crook. "You can leave right now...and go straight to jail."

Comprehension Cliffhangers: Mysteries © 2010 by Bill Doyle, Scholastic Inc.

Loot Lookers

Sincerely, Sinister

Background Building

The Loot Lookers, Natalie and Harry, make up a crime-solving team. Ask students to list other instances where authors present a kid team of two or more main characters. Possible answers include characters in series such as Harry Potter, The Chronicles of Narnia, and Magic Tree House.

Have students consider why authors might choose to write about a team of main characters rather than just one main hero. Possible benefits include: with more characters, authors have a greater chance of appealing to a wider audience, such as boys *and* girls; the main characters talking back and forth can convey story points through dialogue; or, with multiple heroes, there can be different perspectives.

Focus of Reading Strategy:
Analyzing Character

As they read, have students take a close look at the characters of Mr. Bellford, Mrs. Bellford, and their son, Frederick. Encourage students to pay attention to the way the characters interact with one another as a family. Do they make a realistic family unit?

After Reading

Talk About It

Return to the discussion of character. Did students find the Bellfords to be a believable family? Ask what could have been added, changed, or deleted to give the characters more dimension.

Write About It

Discuss with students if they think Mr. and Mrs. Bellford seem grateful for the work Natalie and Harry did for them. Have students pretend they are either Mr. or Mrs. Bellford and write a thank-you note to the Loot Lookers for a job well done. Point out that students should consider the kind of language the sometimes snooty Bellfords might use.

Vocabulary

Here's a list of words your students will come across in this mystery—as well as their definitions:

forgery	illegal copy of something
indignities	losses of dignity or self-esteem
intricate	complex
malfunctioned	failed to work correctly
miserably	showing unhappiness
penthouse	expensive apartment on the top floor
previous	occurring before
sabotage	damage property deliberately
shattered	broke
sneered	showed contempt or scorn
snooty	displaying a haughty manner
supposedly	as some people believe
suspiciously	indicating a belief that something is wrong
tousled	ruffled
whapped	struck

Sincerely, Sinister

Discovered in a luxurious penthouse, a hidden note paints Harry and Natalie into a mysterious corner.

Harry and Natalie, 12-year-old founders of the Loot Lookers Detective Agency, arrived at the Bellfords' penthouse apartment just around 7 P.M. on Monday. As they stood in the entrance hall shaking the snow off their clothes, a butler and a maid were busy cleaning up broken glass and a few pieces of wood off the floor.

"What's going on here—" Harry started to ask, when he lost control of his soggy glove that he was tugging off one hand. The glove flew a few feet and whapped the butler in the head with a wet, squishy sound. "Sorry!" Harry cried.

"Really, children should be more careful," the butler sneered, ignoring the apology. "First, I trip on a wire in the room of the one who *lives* here, and now these two ragamuffins arrive and fling wet garments at me. Indignities know no end!"

Natalie could see that they should get right down to business. "We're here to see Mr. and Mrs. Bellford. They called us with a case and asked us to come over right away."

The butler eyed them suspiciously for a moment, but finally told the maid to show them to the library. Harry and Natalie followed her down a long hallway.

"I don't even know what the mystery is," Harry said, relieved to be away from the angry butler's stare, "but I bet the butler did it."

Natalie was laughing at the joke as the maid ushered them into the library and returned to the front hall. The Loot Lookers were not alone in the room. Mr. and Mrs. Bellford were leaning over a desk. They were signing what looked to be a spelling quiz that had been graded with an F.

"Harry! Natalie!" Mrs. Bellford called. Rushing over to them, she kissed the air on either side of both their faces. Mrs. Bellford could be a little snooty, but Natalie liked her. She treated the Loot Lookers like they were adults. Mrs. Bellford followed Natalie's gaze to the quiz on the desk.

"Oh," she said. "I'm afraid our son, Frederick, didn't do so well on his quiz. The teacher has asked us to sign it."

Mr. Bellford walked over to shake hands with Natalie and Harry. "Not to worry. Our little third grader is quite the student these days. In fact, Frederick is studying for his big test on African countries tomorrow."

As if on cue, Frederick came into the room. "Actually, I'm right here, Father." He looked at Harry and Natalie and said, "You're the Loot Lookers and supposedly great detectives. But I'll bet you'll never guess what we've discovered."

Natalie smiled. "Something to do with a painting, right?"

"How on Earth did you know that?" Mr. Bellford asked, stunned.

Chuckling, Harry answered for her. "It doesn't take Sherlock Holmes to notice the shattered glass and the wood of a broken frame in the front hall. Both are used to hang paintings."

"Very good!" Mrs. Bellford said. "Yes, a painting fell in the front hall. And it was by the famous artist Sinister Van Gloop. Or so we thought."

Natalie realized they were getting ahead of themselves. She liked to get the facts of the case in order. "Please, start at the beginning. What happened? Why did you call us here?"

Everyone sat down on the leather couches, and Mrs. Bellford told the story. "My husband's hobby is flying small, remote-controlled planes—even indoors. In fact, every evening he flies one down the hallway to Frederick's room. It's the signal that tells Frederick it's time for dinner. I always told my husband that toy would cause damage. And I was right!"

Mr. Bellford held out his hands as if to say he was blameless. "Something malfunctioned. The plane wouldn't turn when it reached the end of the hall, and it struck the painting. The painting crashed to the floor, and that's when we found this taped to the back of it." Mr. Bellford handed Natalie a letter. Harry leaned in so he could read it as well. This was what the letter said:

To Whomever Should Find This Letter,

This may not be the first letter I have ever written, but first letters can be very important, don't you think?

I have hidden this note behind this painting for a very good reason. This painting is not authentic. It is a copy. I have hidden the real painting. And the only way to find it is to solve this riddle of the letter.

My only regret rests on concealing content, obviously. Let this first-letter rule apply to my last sentence—and be all the punishment I endure.

Sincerely,
Sinister Van Gloop

"Very interesting," Harry murmured, sitting back on the couch.

"I'm glad you think so," Mr. Bellford said, a little sarcastically. "This note says the painting is hidden somewhere. That means the painting we spent three million dollars on is a forgery! It's a fake!"

To calm her husband, Mrs. Bellford put a hand on his arm. She said in a quieter voice, "We paid for a Sinister Van Gloop painting. We want you to help us crack the riddle and find the real one."

Natalie glanced over at Harry with a smile. "It's easy, right?" she said. Harry smiled back and nodded.

"It is?" Mr. Bellford asked. Sarcasm had turned to surprise.

"Sure," Harry said. "According to this note, your painting is in Morocco."

Her eyes wide, Mrs. Bellford said, "How on Earth did you figure that out?"

"We just need to look at the final line of the note," Natalie explained. "There, the writer tells us to look at the previous sentence. He tells us to apply the first-letter rule. Earlier, he told us first letters are very important."

"In other words," Harry chimed in, seeing the Bellfords weren't quite following, "he's telling us to take the first letter of each word in the second-to-last sentence."

"If you do that, you get..." Natalie looked back at the note and spelled out, "M-O-R-R-O-C-C-O."

"Morocco!" Mr. Bellford cried.

"Well, kind of..." Natalie said, and Harry added, "But the word is mis—"

But the Bellfords weren't listening. "Morocco!" Mrs. Bellford exclaimed

Comprehension Cliffhangers: Mysteries © 2010 by Bill Doyle, Scholastic Inc.

happily. "How wonderful! We'll take the jet to Morocco immediately."

Frederick spoke for the first time in a few minutes. "What about school tomorrow, Mummy?" he asked with concern.

Mrs. Bellford patted her son's head. "Poor thing, you'll have to miss it. But this trip seems like a much more educational experience, don't you think?"

Frowning, Mr. Bellford asked, "But where exactly is the real painting hidden? Morocco is a pretty big country."

Natalie held up her hand like a volunteer. "We can take you there."

"Excellent!" Mrs. Bellford said. "I'll call your parents, and you'll fly on our jet with us."

"Oh, that won't be necessary," Natalie said. "I can take you to the other painting, and it will be a short trip. I can show you where it is this very second."

And with that, Natalie walked over and tapped Frederick's head. "It's right here."

Stop Here!

Discussion Questions

1. What has been broken in the hallway? What caused it to break?

2. What was discovered behind the painting? Who do the Bellfords think left the item there?

3. Why have the Bellfords asked Natalie and Harry to come to their penthouse?

4. What do you know about the character of Frederick? How old is he? How does he do in school? Why do you think Natalie taps his head when Mr. Bellford asks about the location of the painting?

OKAY! Keep reading to see if you were able to crack the case!

"What do you mean?" Mrs. Bellford asked with a little laugh. "You think the painting is in Frederick's head?"

"That's right," Harry agreed. "The other painting is in Frederick's head. All of this sprang from his imagination."

"Mummy!" Frederick whined and clutched at his mother.

"What are you saying?" Mrs. Bellford said protectively.

"Frederick wrote the note," Harry said. "He made up the whole thing."

The boy pushed away from his mother. "That's ridiculous!" he said, his voice suddenly loud and angry. "And even if I had, how could I know that the plane would crash into it? That note could have stayed behind the painting forever."

Harry explained, "When we first came in, the butler told us he had stepped on a wire in Frederick's bedroom. I will bet that that wire came from your remote-controlled plane, Mr. Bellford. That's why it malfunctioned."

"Did you sabotage my plane, Frederick?" Mr. Bellford said. "But why?"

Frederick didn't answer, so Natalie did for him. "So that it would fly straight into the painting and knock it to the ground. He knew you would find the note then, and no one would make the connection to him."

"But anyone in this house could have done that!" Frederick shouted.

Shaking her head, Natalie said, "But no one else has the trouble spelling that Frederick does. We saw that he received an F on his last spelling quiz. And in the note's riddle he misspelled Morocco. He added an extra *r*."

This last fact seemed to convince Mrs. Bellford. "Why did you do it, Frederick?"

"Why don't you tell them, Frederick?" Harry said. "It has to do with tomorrow and your exam, doesn't it?"

Frederick still didn't say anything. But this time, he nodded.

His parents gasped. "All this to get out of taking an exam?" Mrs. Bellford asked.

"I didn't want to fail again," said Frederick miserably.

"If you spent as much time actually studying as you do plotting out these intricate plans, you'd get an A on all your exams," Mr. Bellford said sternly. Then, softening at the sight of tears in his son's eyes, he tousled Frederick's hair affectionately.

This must have made Frederick think everything was okay because he asked, "Can we still go to Morocco tonight?"

"For the answer to that," Mrs. Bellford said, "I have an easy word to spell. It has only two letters."

"Let me guess," Natalie said, giving Harry a wink. "That word starts with *n* and ends with *o*."

Comprehension Cliffhangers: Mysteries © 2010 by Bill Doyle, Scholastic Inc.

Loot Lookers

The Unfortunate Fortune

Before Reading

Background Building

This mystery takes place underwater onboard a sunken ship called the *Gigantic*. Authors will often play off well-known events, landmarks, or vehicles (in this case, the *Titanic*) as a kind of shorthand. It's a quick way to set the stage and evoke a mood.

To help students imagine the story's setting, ask them to share what they know about sunken ships. What would they expect to find? How would they explore them? Consider asking them to do research online. Possible famous sunken ships to research include: *Titanic*, *USS Monitor*, *Lusitania*, *Andrea Doria*, and *Yorktown*.

Focus of Reading Strategy:
Making Predictions

From the title, ask what students expect the mystery to be about. Remind them that the action takes place on a sunken ship. Does this setting change their predictions?

After Reading

Talk About It

The poem in this mystery contained clues to finding the treasure behind one of three doors. Ask students to go through the poem line by line, discussing the meaning of each. Have students pick which line they think was the most important to cracking the case. Point to the second line, which leads readers to the word *left*.

Write About It

In this fun exercise, explain that Natalie and Harry are hoping to expand their Loot Lookers business. In fact, they're hiring a new detective. Have students pretend they are applying for the job. What important things will they need to describe about themselves to get the job of detective?

Vocabulary

Here's a list of words your students will come across in this mystery—as well as their definitions:

collision	act of two objects hitting each other
crackle	sharp snapping or popping sound
crevasse	deep crack
desperately	displaying near-hopelessness and anxiety
err	make a mistake
gaping	wide open
hulking	huge
leisure	relaxed manner
measure	way of evaluating something
restraining	holding back
sheepish	showing embarrassment as a result of having done something wrong
signaled	indicated
suspicious	inclined to believe something is wrong or people have shady motives

The Unfortunate Fortune

The depths of the ocean hold the secrets of the world's largest—and most unlucky—diamond.

Desperately, Natalie dove deeper and deeper into the murky ocean. Bubbles from her air tank circled her diving mask and flew past her flippers up toward the surface like a swarm of angry bees. As she swam even faster, her underwater flashlight lit up the hulking shape of the sunken ship about 30 feet below.

The ship was the *Gigantic*, a cruise liner that had once traveled between Europe and the United States carrying wealthy passengers. An iceberg had torn a gaping hole in its hull and sent it to the ocean floor 40 years ago. But it wouldn't stay put much longer. Even now, strong underwater currents caused by a recent earthquake were pushing it toward a mile-deep crevasse. Soon it would be gone forever.

The loss of the ship was bad enough. What was absolutely terrifying was that Natalie's partner and friend, Harry, was trapped on the *Gigantic*. He had swum onboard in search of the famous McGrogan Diamond.

It was the largest diamond in the world and had passed from generation to generation of the McGrogan family—but it seemed to be cursed. In the early 1900s, a train carrying it had derailed and plunged over a cliff. When the diamond was recovered years later, it had been put on a plane, but the plane skidded off the runway at takeoff. Finally, Lester McGrogan had brought it with him onto the *Gigantic*. And then, thanks to the collision with the iceberg, the mighty ship had sunk, taking the diamond down to the bottom of the ocean.

Lester McGrogan's grandchildren wanted to recover the diamond, sell it, and use the money to build a children's hospital. They had hired the Loot Lookers, Natalie and Harry, to find the diamond for them.

So, about an hour ago—after weeks of training—Natalie and Harry had taken out their own boat, which now bobbed on the surface. They had put on diving gear, lowered themselves into the icy water, and dove toward the ocean floor to look for the famous McGrogan Diamond.

Once they had reached the sunken *Gigantic*, Natalie and Harry had floated outside, peering through the tear in the hull into the President's Cabin. This is where the diamond was supposed to be located. But it wasn't going to be easy to find. The diamond's streak of bad luck had made Lester McGrogan, the man who carried the diamond onto the *Gigantic*, suspicious of everything and everyone. And he had hidden the diamond behind one of three doors that lined the back of the cabin.

According to McGrogan family legend, if you opened the wrong door, the diamond would be lost forever. Luckily, the McGrogans who hired Natalie and Harry had found a riddle written by Lester McGrogan. They were certain it held a clue. It read:

> *For those who seek glittering treasure,*
> *Past of leave is the measure.*
> *Remember to enter at one's leisure,*
> *To err in this leads to no pleasure!*

Not sure what it meant, Natalie had thought a lot about the riddle. She was still thinking about it when they had arrived at the *Gigantic* just a short time ago.

"Let's go in," Harry had said, speaking through the radios in their diving equipment and pulling her out of her thoughts. Harry had looked ready to swim through the tear in the ship's hull and into the President's Cabin.

But Natalie shook her head. "No, wait." She had been checking out the current and how the *Gigantic* was slipping closer to the edge of the crevasse. At that moment, she knew it was too dangerous to go inside. If they were in there when the ship went over the edge and plummeted down one mile to the bottom of the pit, they would die.

Natalie had decided they would have to give up. Yes, the diamond would be lost, and the hospital would never be built. But they had no choice. She had signaled that they should return to the surface. It was the only safe thing to do. But then, halfway back up to the top, Natalie had realized that Harry was no longer swimming next to her. She had looked back down in time to see Harry's fins disappear into the *Gigantic*.

"Harry!" Natalie had shouted over her radio. "Get back out here now!"

"I have to find the diamond," Harry had radioed from inside the President's Cabin, where Natalie couldn't see him. "It's too important to let it go."

So Natalie had started swimming back down, just as she heard the sound of a door opening and closing inside the cabin and then a crashing sound.

"Harry? Harry!" she had yelled over her radio. But there had been no response. Harry was stuck somewhere in the *Gigantic*. And Natalie had to find him before the ship went over the edge of the crevasse—or they both ran out of air.

Natalie had just slipped through the hole in the hull into the President's Cabin when there was a crackle over her radio. "Harry?" Natalie cried. "Is that you?"

There was more static, and then she could hear Harry's voice. "Natalie…" He sounded woozy and really out of it. "I rushed through the door. I didn't enter at my 'leisure.' A beam must have fallen and hit my head and messed up my radio. I can't see a thing—"

"Where are you?" Natalie asked, cutting him off and looking at the three doors in front of her. The swirling sea had erased any signs of Harry passing through one of them. "Which door?"

"I solved the riddle. It's the second line—" But before he could tell her, his radio went dead.

"Don't worry," Natalie said, in case he could still hear her. "I'll find you."

But, to be honest, Natalie wasn't so sure she could.

She gazed at the three doors on the back wall—left, right, and center. If she chose the wrong door, the others might never open no matter how hard she tried. Then she'd never be able to rescue Harry. She had to get it right the first time.

What had Harry said before his radio went dead? Something about the second line? She recalled the second line of the riddle: *Past of leave is the measure.*

She wondered hopelessly how that would help her decide to open the left, right, or center door.

And that's when the answer hit her. "Yes!" she said out loud. "That must be it!"

Without hesitating, she reached out for one of the doorknobs.

Comprehension Cliffhangers: Mysteries © 2010 by Bill Doyle, Scholastic Inc.

Discussion Questions

1. What is the *Gigantic*? Where is it located and how did it get there? Will it stay where it is forever?

2. What are Natalie and Harry looking for? Why do some people think that it has a curse on it? Give two reasons.

3. What is a written clue that Natalie and Harry have to help them in the search? Where did it come from?

4. Which door do you think Natalie is reaching for? Can you guess why she seems so certain about which door to choose?

OKAY! **Keep reading to see if you were able to crack the case!**

The metal doorknob of the left door turned under Natalie's hand. She had to force herself not to shove it open as quickly as possible. The riddle said to move at her leisure. Finally, it was open. She shone her flashlight around the small inner room and instantly spotted Harry. He was trapped under a steel beam.

"Harry!" she cried. She was able to shove the beam off of him and pull him out. "Are you okay?"

He tapped his head to tell her his radio didn't work, but then gave her a thumbs-up to let her know he was uninjured.

They made their way out of the *Gigantic* and swam to the surface. Back on the deck of their own boat, they removed their masks and air tanks. The crew handed them towels. As they were warming up, Harry said to Natalie, "Okay, before you yell at me for going in there on my own, tell me one thing. How did you know to go through the left door?"

Forcing herself to remain calm, Natalie answered, "I heard you say something about the second line before your radio went dead."

Nodding, Harry said, "The second line of the riddle was the key: *Past of leave is the measure.*"

"I thought about that line," Natalie said. "What is the past of *leave*? The answer is *left*. The verb *left* is the past tense of *leave*. So I knew it must be the *left* door."

"And, lucky for me, you figured it out," Harry said. Then, lowering his head as if getting ready to be tackled, he added, "All right, let me have it."

Natalie stopped restraining herself. "Harry!" she yelled, giving him a whap across the head. "I could kill you for risking your life like that!"

Shrugging, Harry looked sheepish and sorry. "Okay, it was pretty stupid. I won't do it again. I promise."

Natalie wasn't done yelling, though. "No fortune is worth that kind of risk!"

"So . . ." Harry said, looking up and meeting her eyes. "I guess you're not interested in this thing I found behind the left door." He held out his hand. Sitting on his palm, glittering in the afternoon sun, was the McGrogan Diamond.

"If you're not interested," Harry said, laughing at Natalie's happy, shocked expression. "I guess I could just toss it back in the ocean. Or maybe it can be used to build that children's hospital!"

Monumental Mysteries

Tower of Trouble

Before Reading

Background Building

This mystery takes place at a famous landmark. Ask students to share what they know about the Eiffel Tower. Erected between 1886 and 1889 and located in Paris, France, the Eiffel Tower is a 984-foot-tall construction of lattice-worked iron that is:

❖ named for its builder, Alexandre-Gustave Eiffel

❖ able to sway about four inches in any direction in strong winds

❖ visited by thousands of tourists each year

❖ equipped with elevators, observation decks, and restaurants for visitors

Focus of Reading Strategy:
Understanding Cause and Effect

Discuss with students how a cause makes something happen. An effect is what happens. For example, flicking a switch causes the effect of a light coming on. While they read this story, ask students to keep an eye out for the cause that they think leads to the biggest effect.

After Reading

Talk About It

This story has a *red herring*. Explain to students that a red herring is a device used by mystery writers to throw the reader off track and build up to a bigger surprise ending. In this mystery, Mark accuses the supermodel of being the cat burglar. Ask students if this red herring helps the story. How?

Write About It

As students might have noticed while reading this mystery, Paris is sometimes called the City of Lights. The city earned this nickname in the 1800s when gas lamps were first used to light one of its famous roadways. Ask students to give nicknames to their own city or town. What nicknames would they give to other cities?

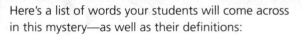

Vocabulary

Here's a list of words your students will come across in this mystery—as well as their definitions:

blasé	not impressed
blurry	unclear
bonjour	French for "good day" or "hello"
canine	pointed tooth
gaped	stared with open-mouthed wonder
lurch	sudden movement to the side
observation deck	platform in a high location with a broad view
pitched	fell
sacre bleu	French, similar to "holy cow"
sympathetically	in a friendly way that shows understanding
tremendous	extremely large
wafted	floated gently

Tower of Trouble

Trapped in an elevator high over the city of Paris, a young detective faces danger on the way up.

"*Bonjour*," said the elevator operator, greeting the seven passengers in French as they squeezed into the cramped space. After the doors slid shut behind them, the elevator began its long climb with a little jolt. And just like that, they were heading up the side of the Eiffel Tower!

Thirteen-year-old Mark could hardly believe that he was actually in Paris, France. Growing up in Ohio, Mark had always dreamed of visiting the Eiffel Tower and the other sites of Paris. Now here he was with his Uncle Rob and Aunt Kay, going up the tower itself. Soon they would be at the observation deck, 911 feet above the City of Lights!

Aunt Kay was snapping photos of Paris through the windows of the elevator, and the other members of the tour were saying things like "Fantastic!" and "How wonderful!" Mark and his aunt and uncle had been traveling around Paris with the same people from a tour group for the past week. So Mark knew the other elevator passengers pretty well by now.

The Italian woman named Signora Gala was standing by a window with a bored look on her face. She was a supermodel, and was very tall and had shaved her head completely bald. She gazed out, trying to act blasé, but Mark could see she was excited.

Three other people were also on the elevator: a Japanese businessman named Mr. Hiroshi, an American dentist who introduced himself as Dr. Franks, and a Spanish writer named Señor Ricci. Unlike Signora Gala, they didn't try to hide how thrilled they were.

The elevator operator smiled. He obviously enjoyed hearing passengers *ooh* and *aah* over the ever-expanding view as they went up and up.

Then, suddenly, the operator gave a start and his smile vanished. "*Sacre bleu!*" he whispered, which was like saying "Holy cow!" in English.

Mark felt a twinge of fear. Was something wrong?

The operator's eyes went to a small poster that had been taped near the elevator controls, and then he gaped at the passengers. He was looking at someone in the elevator, but because they were all so jammed together, Mark couldn't tell whom.

The poster was a few feet away. Mark could only make out a blurry sketch of someone and the top two lines. It said:

WANTED!

Cat Burglar of Paris

Still gawking at one of the passengers, the elevator operator gasped in English, "It's you! The Cat Burglar of Paris!"

Then the operator's face turned bright red, and he pitched backward. He slammed into the elevator controls, snapping off part of the control handle and falling to the floor. There was a tremendous lurch as the elevator jerked to a sudden halt. The elevator car was now at a complete standstill, about 500 feet off the ground!

The passengers screamed in four different languages—English, Japanese, Spanish, and Italian. Even the supermodel couldn't pretend to be bored anymore. Everyone started shoving around the small space, looking for an emergency exit. But there was no way out. They were trapped.

"I'm a doctor!" Dr. Franks shouted above everyone else. "Stand back and let me examine this man." Everyone quieted down as the dentist crouched next to the elevator operator. After a moment, Dr. Franks looked up. "This man has fainted, probably from some kind of shock."

"There's blood!" said Mr. Hiroshi. He was pointing at two small drops of blood on the man's chin. Mark bent so he could see. The operator must have bitten his lip when he fell.

"It's just from his canine," Mark told the others.

Dr. Franks laughed. "Don't be ridiculous, Mark. There isn't a dog in here."

No dog, Mark thought, but growing panic. Most passengers were looking with frightened eyes out the windows down at the Parisian streets far, far below. Mark could feel the elevator moving from side to side as the Eiffel Tower swayed in the strong wind.

Trying to sound calm, Mark said, "We're stuck here until the elevator operator wakes up and fixes the controls. Or until the operator at the bottom overrides the controls and starts us moving again."

"What happened? Why did the man faint?" asked Aunt Kay, her hands fluttering nervously about like birds darting in the air. Uncle Rob put an arm around her shoulders to comfort her.

Mark played back the last few minutes in his head. "The elevator operator was looking at one of us when he fainted. I think he recognized the Cat Burglar of Paris described on the poster."

"What poster?" Mr. Hiroshi asked.

When Mark went to show them, he could see that the poster had been torn. In all the confusion, someone had ripped the sketch of the Cat Burglar of Paris off the poster. To destroy it, Mark guessed. But at least half of the poster was still intact and held a brief note and description.

Translating French to English, Mark read the message to the others. "'To all elevator operators: Keep a lookout! The Cat Burglar of Paris is a dangerous criminal who has been stealing diamonds and jewels from the finest houses in Paris for the past week. Only one person has seen the Cat Burglar and has described the thief as tall, bald, thin, bearded, and elderly.'"

"We've been in Paris a week, like the Cat Burglar, but otherwise that doesn't describe any of us," said Señor Ricci. He was the only one who didn't look nervous. "Why don't we just wait for the elevator operator to wake up? I'm sure this was all just a misunderstanding."

"I agree," chimed in Dr. Franks. "Besides, the Cat Burglar is supposed to be dangerous. No one on this elevator looks like a dangerous person."

Looks can be deceiving, Mark thought, but instead he said, "Someone on this elevator is not who he or she claims to be. We need to figure out who the Cat Burglar is before the elevator starts again and takes us to the top. Once the doors

Comprehension Cliffhangers: Mysteries © 2010 by Bill Doyle, Scholastic Inc.

open, the crook might escape."

The supermodel Signora Gala cocked an eyebrow at him. "And how, little boy, are we going to figure out which one of us is the criminal?" All eyes turned to Mark.

Blushing slightly at all the attention, he said, "We'll take a look at the four possible suspects."

"But there are seven passengers, dear," Aunt Kay said. "Aren't we all suspects?"

"Not really, Aunt Kay," Mark answered. "I know it's not you or Uncle Rob. And it's not me. That leaves Señor Ricci, Signora Gala, Dr. Franks, and Mr. Hiroshi. We'll see if the adjectives from the description match anyone onboard the elevator." Mark paused to read the poster again. "According to this, the Cat Burglar of Paris is tall and thin."

"Mr. Hiroshi is tall," Uncle Rob said.

"True," Mark agreed. "But he's not terribly thin." When Mr. Hiroshi started to protest, Mark added, "Sorry!"

Mark quickly moved on. "And Señor Ricci and Dr. Franks are tall and skinny. But neither is bald. So that eliminates them as suspects. That leaves just one person as a prime suspect."

"So who is it?" Signora Gala asked, touching her hairless head and sounding bored again.

Mark turned to her. "You," he said.

There was a moment of shocked silence. Then Signora Gala cried, "No, I am innocent!"

Rubbing his beard, Dr. Franks glared at her. "That's what they all say."

"But how can it be me?" Signora Gala asked. "I'm tall and bald, but I don't match the whole description. You forgot that the Cat Burglar has a—"

Just then the elevator gave a mighty lurch. They were all thrown to the side as the car continued its climb to the top. Someone down below must have started them moving again.

Seconds later, the doors opened onto the top observatory deck of the Eiffel Tower. Two young French security guards were standing nearby.

"Guards, take this woman into custody!" Dr. Franks said, jerking a thumb at Signora Gala. "She is the Cat Burglar of Paris!"

But Mark held up his hands to stop them. "No, leave her alone. She's not the one. The Cat Burglar is actually right there!"

Mark pointed directly at one of the other elevator passengers.

Stop Here!

Discussion Questions

1. Where does much of the action take place during this mystery? Do you think that's a good spot for a mystery? Why?

2. How many people are suspects? Can you name them?

3. What is the description of the Cat Burglar of Paris? Does that description match any of the suspects?

4. When Mark exits the elevator, he seems to change his mind about the identity of the crook. Why would Mark accuse someone he knew was innocent of being the Cat Burglar? Who do you think is the real crook?

OKAY! **Now keep reading to see if your predictions were correct!**

Seeing Mark pointing at him, Dr. Franks shouted, "You'll never catch me!" Shoving his way past the other passengers, he made a break for it. Or tried to.

Uncle Rob stuck out his foot, and Dr. Franks tripped and fell right into the arms of the guards. As Dr. Franks stumbled, the wig he'd been wearing flew from his head. It wafted over the railing and out into the Parisian air, looking like a wounded bird trying to fly.

A few minutes later, one guard held the bald Dr. Franks while the other searched his bag. The elevator operator had awakened and was leaning against the railing of the observatory, speaking with a French official.

On the other side of the observatory deck, Aunt Kay looked at Mark. "How on Earth did you know the Cat Burglar was Dr. Franks?"

"And why did you accuse me?" Signora Gala demanded. "As I was trying to say, the description said the Cat Burglar of Paris has a beard. I certainly don't have one of those! I'm a supermodel, for heaven's sake!"

"I'm sorry, Signora Gala," Mark said. "Really, I am. I knew the Cat Burglar could be dangerous. I wanted the real crook to think he was safe. I didn't want him to cause any trouble while we were all still trapped on the elevator."

"But how did you know?" Aunt Kay asked again.

"When I mentioned to Dr. Franks that the operator's cut lip came from his canine," Mark explained, "he thought I was talking about a dog. But if he were really a dentist, he would have known I was talking about the front tooth called the canine. So I knew he was faking about being a dentist."

"Oh!" Uncle Rob said, impressed. "Good work, Mark."

Smiling from the praise, Mark took a quick look around the observatory deck. Unfortunately, a fog had rolled in, obscuring much of the Paris skyline below.

"Are you disappointed about the fog blocking the view?" Aunt Kay asked, touching his arm sympathetically.

"No way!" Mark said. He was watching the guards lead Dr. Franks away in handcuffs. "This is best view I think anyone's ever had from the Eiffel Tower!"

Curse of the Mummy's Daddy

Before Reading

Background Building

What's at stake in a story can generate suspense and make the reader care more about the outcome. Explain to students that stakes represent what is up for grabs or what is risked. For example, in a detective story about a missing puppy, the stakes are high: Will the private eye track down the cute pooch? On the other hand, in a mystery about a missing paper clip, the stakes are low, and the story is not as interesting.

Ask students about the stakes in a favorite mystery book, movie, or TV show. Now point out that in this story, the stakes are life and death.

Focus of Reading Strategy: Making Predictions

Read students the title of this mystery, "Curse of the Mummy's Daddy." Ask them to use what they know about other mummy mysteries to predict what this story will be about. Where will it take place? Who might be some of the characters? Now have them read the story to see if their predictions are on track.

After Reading

Talk About It

Some authors write according to a "rule of three." In this mystery, there are three doors blocking the way out. Ask students why they think the writer chose to have three doors in this story. Would two have been enough to build tension? Would four or more have been overkill?

Write About It

Chances are your students have seen shows about mummies. Ask them to think of this story like a movie. Have students storyboard the action, paying close attention to the suspenseful scene where Sarah opens the final door. Point out that including sound effects will make the storyboards even more exciting to read.

Vocabulary

Here's a list of words your students will come across in this mystery—as well as their definitions:

archaeological	relating to archaeology, the scientific study of ancient cultures
authentic	genuine
device	tool
gnarled	twisted
hieroglyphs	symbols used to represent objects, sounds, or concepts
logic	reasoning
panicking	feeling overwhelming fear
pharaohs	ancient Egyptian kings
rumbling	loud, dull, continuous sound
sphinx	statue built by the ancient Egyptians
tantrums	displays of bad temper
translates	rewords from one language into another

Curse of the Mummy's Daddy

Deep in a forgotten palace, Sarah, who has dreamt of being part of a mystery, is about to see her dream turn into a nightmare.

Sarah was the biggest mystery fan in her fifth-grade class back in Los Angeles. She read every detective story she could get her hands on, and she went to see all the new *Inspector Marvel* movies on the first day. She was an authentic mystery nut!

So you might think she would be happy to find herself smack in the middle of a mystery in the Valley of the Pharaohs in Egypt. But you'd be wrong. Because this mystery was scarier than any she had ever read about or seen on the big screen.

It had all started that morning when Sarah arrived at an archaeological dig site to explore a newly discovered ancient palace. Buried beneath the sand for three thousand years, it had once been home to mighty pharaohs. Her dad, Dr. Robbins, was the head archaeologist in charge of carefully digging up the palace so it could be studied by researchers. Sarah couldn't have been more proud.

When Sarah and her dad reached the site out in the desert at 6 A.M., the other members of the dig team hadn't arrived yet. So it was just Sarah and her dad as they made their way into the half-buried palace.

"Be careful not to touch anything, okay?" Dr. Robbins warned her as they ducked through a narrow stone entryway. "Most of the building is still under 20 feet of desert sand. And there might be all sorts of hidden traps and secret doors that we know nothing about yet."

"I'll be careful, Dad," Sarah assured him. "Don't worry."

Sarah's father led her through the ancient structure, the beams of their flashlights bouncing off one magnificent sight after another. Brightly painted hieroglyphs covered many walls, and dramatic sculptures of Egyptian gods stood in corners.

Then they entered a room about the size of a small bedroom. There were no windows and a single doorway. In the center of the room stood a column of stacked clay bricks with a strange stone on the top. Unlike in the other rooms, there were no symbols or hieroglyphs on the walls.

"What *is* this place?" Sarah asked, walking around the brick column to get a better look at the stone.

Grinning with excitement, Dr. Robbins said, "It's the center of an ancient mystery. The Pharaoh would send his only son here when he was bad or disrespectful."

"Kind of a like time-out room, huh?" Sarah said with a laugh. It was hard to imagine kings and queens dealing with everyday problems like temper tantrums. "Did the son become a pharaoh?" she asked.

"Yes," Dr. Robbins told her. "The son's name translates into English literally as Pullturnknock."

Chuckling, Sarah said, "Wow, that name's quite a mouthful."

"Well, he was quite a *hand*ful," Dr. Robbins said. "When he would throw a tantrum, he was locked in here. It was a way of teaching him patience and logic."

Sarah was confused. "How could a room teach him anything?"

"Look closely at that stone on top of the bricks," Dr. Robbins said. "That's a control device that would unlock the door. The stone on top can move in different directions. If you move it around the right way, the door opens."

"Wow," Sarah said. "I'm glad you never sent me to a room like this."

"Actually, this is giving me a few ideas," Dr. Robbins said, pretending to be

Comprehension Cliffhangers: Mysteries © 2010 by Bill Doyle, Scholastic Inc.

inspired. "We might want to do some remodeling when we get back home."

Sarah laughed again and, without thinking about it, leaned against a wall. She felt something shift—and she knew in a flash she had just set off a hidden trap. Before she could shout out a warning, the room started shaking.

Suddenly, a stone door came crashing down, blocking the only doorway out of the room. Another door fell in front of the first. And then one more!

Wham! Wham! Wham!

The three massive doors slammed into place one in front of the other, sending tremors through the whole room. A crack in the ceiling opened up, and a piece of stone the size of a flat-screen TV fell on Dr. Robbins's legs, and he let out a little cry.

"Dad!" Sarah shouted, and rushed to him. With the doorway closed, their flashlights were the only light in the room. She crouched down next to him. "Are you okay?"

"I think so." His hands were free and he tried pushing the stone off his legs. "Nothing's broken or anything. But we need to get out of here."

Sarah could see what he meant. Desert sand was pouring down into the room through the cracked ceiling. Right onto Dr. Robbins. In just a few minutes, her father would be buried under the sand.

Together, Sarah and Dr. Robbins tried to shove the stone. But with the added weight of sand falling from above, it was too heavy. Sarah had to do something.

"How do I open the door, Dad?" she asked desperately.

"I'm not sure, Sarah," Dr. Robbins said. "No one knows how to use the control device. We only know that if you move the stone incorrectly, the room will stay locked. Back then, Pullturnknock's father might have come in from the outside to let him out. But now..."

He didn't need to finish the sentence. Sarah knew she had to crack the mystery of Pullturnknock before her dad got buried in sand.

She walked over to the doorway and flashed her light on the first stone door that blocked their way out. Unlike the walls, the door had a symbol on it. It was a drawing of the sun rising.

"That must be a clue as to how to use the control device!" she said. But she couldn't think what the clue might mean. Her mind was all over the place.

She knew she was panicking. She thought of what her dad had said. Pullturnknock had had to calm down to think his way out. Sarah had to do the same.

Stop freaking out, she told herself.

How could she move the stone control device so that it moved like the sun?

She took a chance and pulled on the stone like she was pulling up the sun. There was a deep rumbling sound, and the first door slid into the ground.

She'd done it!

"Good job," her dad said. "There are still two more doors to go. You can do it, Sarah!"

When the first stone door slid away, it had revealed the second stone door. This one had a symbol carved into it as well. It was a picture of a tornado and an old gnarled tree.

"What do they have in common?" Dr. Robbins wondered out loud.

"I know! They're both twisted." Sarah gave the stone a turn.

The second door disappeared into the ground. Sarah looked at her dad and was shocked to see the sand was nearly up to his neck.

"Hang on, Dad," Sarah said. "Just one more door." On the last door, there was a drawing of the head and shoulders of an Egyptian boy. There were also hieroglyphs. "Those hieroglyphs say it's a picture of Pullturnknock," Dr. Robbins said.

"Okay, but there's only one third of him showing in the drawing," Sarah said, feeling her panic rise again. "What does it mean?"

Tilting his mouth up to avoid the sand that was now at his chin, Dr. Robbins said, "We have to think like Pullturnknock!"

Sarah listened to her dad. And then she knew the answer.

Or at least she hoped she did. If she made a mistake, her dad wouldn't be the only one buried in sand. Soon, she would be, too.

Sarah reached a shaking hand toward the stone…

Stop Here! Discussion Questions

1. Where is Sarah from? What country is she in during the action of this story? What does Sarah like to watch and read?

2. What does Sarah's dad do? Why is she so proud of him at the beginning of the story?

3. When Sarah and her dad first enter the palace, what warning does he give her? Do you think she listened to the warning? How did Sarah and her dad get trapped in the room?

4. What did Sarah do to open the first two stone doors? What do you think she should do to open the last door?

OKAY! **Now keep reading to see if you're on the right track.**

The final door rumbled down into the floor. The doorway was now open.

"Yes!" Sarah shouted. Some of the sand rushed out of the room. With the decreased weight of the sand, and with Sarah's help, Dr. Robbins was able to free himself from beneath the stone.

"What did you do?" he asked, once they were safe outside and had given each other hugs. "How did you get us out of there?"

"It was the last picture that really made everything clear to me," Sarah said. "One third of Pullturnknock was on that last door, and there were three doors. I knew there must be a connection, something to do with the number three. So I broke his name down into three parts."

"I don't get it," Dr. Robbins said.

Sarah said, "The first part of Pullturnknock's name means *pull*, like pulling up the sun. The second part is *turn*, like the twisting of a tornado..."

A light flicked on in Dr. Robbins's eyes. "And the last third of his name is *knock*!"

"Pullturn*knock*!" Sarah cried. "I knew I had to knock on the stone to open the final door."

Shaking his head in wonder, Dr. Robbins said, "Pull, turn, knock. That's the key to unlocking the door!"

Watching her dad, Sarah's happiness suddenly turned to guilt. She thought of the mess she had made inside the palace and of the danger she had put her dad in. "Sorry," she said, looking down at the ground.

"Why?" Dr. Robbins said, looking genuinely confused.

Sarah's shoulders slumped. "I almost got you buried alive by leaning against that wall."

"Oh, that?" said Dr. Robbins, like it was no big deal. "You just solved one of the oldest mysteries in Egypt! I'm really proud of you!"

"I'm glad you think so," Sarah said with relief, and gave her dad another hug. "Or should I say, I'm glad you *sphinx* so!"

Monumental Mysteries

Gateway to Mystery

Before Reading

Background Building

Let students know this mystery takes place in a U.S. National Park, specifically, under the Gateway Arch in St. Louis. Ask students if they have been to a national park and to describe their experiences. A quick visit to the National Park Service's Web site at www.nps.gov will help fuel discussion and set the stage for this mystery.

Focus of Reading Strategy: Making Inferences

An inference is an informed guess based on the clues found in a story and on readers' own experiences. Good readers are able to use information in the text and events in their own lives to make reasonable assumptions. Ask students to think about Troy's motives while reading this story. Why do they think he wanted to be the one to discover the family's hidden treasure?

After Reading

Talk About It

This mystery centers on a family legend of hidden treasure. Do any students' families have legends that have been passed down from generation to generation? These legends can include funny stories or tales of heroic deeds. Challenge students to ask their parents or guardians about family legends. Ask for volunteers to share these stories.

Write About It

Have students create two columns on a page. Instruct them to use one column to write down comments about any subject, which can be as mundane as the weather. In the other column, have students rewrite the comments as if they were using Double E's typewriter from the story. In other words, wherever there is the letter *i*, they will replace it with an *e*. Ask students to read their "Double E" comments out loud and see if the rest of the class can figure out what they are saying.

Vocabulary

Here's a list of words your students will come across in this mystery—as well as their definitions:

breathlessly	with intensity
concealed	hid
etched	cut
horizon	line in the distance where land seems to meet the sky
kaleidoscope	colorful, complex, and shifting pattern
kooky	wacky
legend	story that has been passed down from generation to generation
lever	rigid bar that is used to lift something by applying force to one end
reasoning	logical thinking
spectacular	remarkable
stationery	paper for writing letters
testament	old word for a legal will
transferred	passed along

Gateway to Mystery

A family treasure is hidden somewhere in a U.S. National Park. Can Troy crack the case and find it after all these years?

All his life, 10-year-old Troy Evans had been hearing about his family's hidden treasure. According to the will of his grandfather, Eli "Double E" Evans, the treasure was buried somewhere under the Gateway Arch in St. Louis.

Double E had been one of the burly construction workers who built the Gateway Arch, part of a U.S. National Park. He had been up there soaring 630 feet above the ground as the huge span was completed in 1965. On his last day on the job, he concealed the treasure somewhere on the site. He wanted to be sure that future generations of his family would visit the monument.

Over the decades since Double E's death, the legend of the treasure had grown, but no one had been able to find it.

But that didn't stop the Evans clan from talking about it constantly. Every Thanksgiving or Christmas, the whole family gathered at Troy's house in Chicago. During these holidays, they would spend hours talking about the treasure, trying to guess what it was and exactly where it was buried.

They didn't have much of a clue. There was just one line in Double E's will about the treasure. It said:

Look down for the Arch treasure when the summer sun sets en the East.

"Why did he write 'en the East' instead of 'in the East'?" Troy's cousin had asked the last time they were all sitting at the table for Thanksgiving.

"That's easy," Aunt Clara answered, digging into a heap of potatoes. "I think it's because his mother was from Spain. In Spanish, *en* means 'in.' It was just a simple mistake."

"Hmmm," Troy said, sounding unconvinced. "But how can the sun set in the east? It sets in the west."

"Who knows?" Uncle Morty chimed in. "Double E was a little kooky. He was always misspelling stuff. Remember what he called his will? He typed 'Last Well and Testament' instead of 'Last Will and Testament.' No one will ever find that treasure."

But Troy always believed that he would someday solve the mystery.

In fact, a week after Thanksgiving, he had called the U.S. National Park offices in St. Louis. After getting transferred from person to person, he was connected to the national park's director, whose name was Mr. Brandt. Troy explained to him about the treasure.

"Sure," Mr. Brandt said in a deep voice. "I've heard of Double E. My own father knew him, used to say what an interesting fella he was. Double E even told my father about hiding the treasure. Said it was something worth more than anything."

"Did he say where it was?" Troy asked eagerly into the phone.

"No, son, he didn't," Mr. Brandt said. "But he did say something else. Let me see if I can remember exactly what it was." He paused to think. "Double E said, 'One day a special type of family member will come looking for the right key and find the treasure.'" Mr. Brandt paused again and then said, "Troy, maybe that person is you."

That did it! Troy had to visit the Arch so he could find the treasure himself. That spring, for his birthday, Troy asked for one thing: a two-day trip to St. Louis. So, on a beautiful June day, his mom and dad drove him from Chicago to St. Louis, where they checked into a hotel.

After dropping off their luggage, they went to visit the Arch. Now, Troy was standing directly beneath it, gazing up and trying to take it all in.

The Arch was spectacular.

"Pretty amazing, isn't it?" Troy's dad said, also looking up in wonder. "Incredible that our family had something to do with building this monument."

Troy heard the words. But the treasure had been on his mind for so long, and he felt like they were so close, he couldn't think of much else.

"We need to wait for the sun to set," Troy said. "Just like Double E's clue said to do. 'Look down for the Arch treasure when the summer sun sets....' Then we might be able to find the treasure."

It was already past 9 P.M., and as Troy and his parents watched, the sun sank lower and lower in the west, casting a kaleidoscope of pink and red and purple across the St. Louis sky.

Troy scanned the Arch for some kind of clue or indication as to where the treasure might be hidden. But there was nothing. Then the sun was gone.

"We should go back to the hotel," his mom said quietly. Troy shook his head. He didn't want to leave. Not yet.

But a few minutes later, there still weren't any clues. His dad put a hand on his shoulder and said, "Come on, Troy, it's time to go."

Troy felt the weight of disappointment. After all these years of waiting and thinking about it, he couldn't believe that he wasn't going to find the treasure. He wasn't the special family member Double E had predicted, after all. Finally, Troy allowed his mom and dad to lead him away from the Arch.

When they got back to their hotel, there was a package waiting for Troy. It was from Mr. Brandt, the director of the National Park.

"What can that be?" Troy's mom asked. Troy didn't know but he couldn't wait to find out. An envelope was taped to the top of the box. Troy ripped it open and read the letter inside:

Dear Troy,

I called your house in Chicago, and your uncle told me you were staying at this hotel.

We found the item in this box while cleaning out a closet recently in the National Parks office. It belonged to Double E, and he used it to write all of his letters on it.

When you open this box, remember what Double E said: One day a special type of family member will come looking for the right key. I still think that person might be you.

Sincerely,
Mr. Brandt
Director, U.S. National Parks

Troy tore open the box. Inside was an old typewriter. And it had Double E's initials etched into it. E. E. Troy thought about what Mr. Brandt's note said. And about his grandfather's will. The clues started to come together in the back of his mind.

"A special type. The right key," Troy said softly, thinking out loud.

"What did you say?" Troy's dad asked.

But Troy didn't answer. Suddenly, he was too excited. He carried the typewriter over to the desk. Pulling up a chair, he sat down, slid a piece of hotel stationery into the typewriter, and typed a very short note.

"What are you doing, Troy?" his mom and dad asked at the same time. Instead of speaking, Troy handed them the note he had just typed. It read:

E know the answer!

Stop Here! Discussion Questions

1. Who is Double E? Is he still alive? What did he do for a living? Why is he such an important figure to the Evans family? Could his name be a clue to solving the mystery?

2. What does Troy ask for on his birthday? Why is that trip so meaningful to him?

3. When Troy and his parents get back to their hotel, what is waiting there for him? Who sent it? Why do you think the item in the box might be important?

4. What does Troy mean when he types, "E know the answer!"? Can you guess why the 'E' might be a key to cracking the case?

OKAY! **Now keep reading to see if your predictions are on target.**

Early the next morning, even before the sun was up, Troy and his family drove back to the Arch.

"If you solved the mystery, you have to tell us!" his mom said, trying to keep up with him as he strode quickly to the same spot beneath the Arch. Troy had not wanted to disappoint them in case he was wrong. So he waited until they were here to explain what he had figured out last night.

"I think I found the key to finding the treasure," Troy told them breathlessly. "Double E's typewriter was like him. It had two *E*'s."

"I don't get it," his dad said.

Troy took them through his reasoning step by step. "The typewriter doesn't have just one *E* key. In place of the *I* key there's a second *E* key. So every time Double E typed the letter *I*, the letter *E* would show up instead. That's why his last will and testament read 'Last Well and Testament.'"

Troy's mom clapped her hands in excitement. "And that would change the clue about the treasure he left us, too!"

"That clue says, 'Look down for the Arch treasure when the summer sun sets en the East,'" said Troy. "If you change a few of the *E*'s to *I*'s, it says, 'Look

Comprehension Cliffhangers: Mysteries © 2010 by Bill Doyle, Scholastic Inc.

down for the Arch treasure when summer sun *sits in* the East.' Like now!"

Troy pointed to the east, where the sun was just halfway over the horizon as it rose. As the clue directed, Troy kept his head down, looking for something that would tell him where the treasure was hidden.

There! A ray of sunlight bounced off the Arch and reflected down on a brick on a pedestrian walkway below, creating a little point of light. Troy rushed over to it.

"Here it is!" he cried, and crouched down ready to yank out the brick with his bare hands.

"Wait!" his mom called. "Troy! You can't do that!"

Troy stopped. She was right. He couldn't go digging around in a national park. He felt disappointment creeping up on him again, when a deep voice said, "It's okay, Troy, go ahead."

Troy recognized his voice. He looked up to see a big man with a mustache walking toward them. He was wearing a U.S. National Parks uniform.

"Mr. Brandt?" Troy asked, suddenly excited again.

Nodding, the man grinned. "Yes, it's me. I wanted to see if you were the one who would finally solve the mystery. Now go ahead and find the treasure." Mr. Brandt handed him a long, thin piece of steel. "This might help."

Using the steel bar as a lever, Troy carefully lifted the brick. He let out a little gasp. There it was. The family treasure!

It wasn't a bag of money. Or a golden statue. Or diamonds.

It was a folded piece of paper that had yellowed slightly over time. Troy carefully removed it from the hole and unfolded it. He read it and then showed it to his parents.

As they read the note, Troy felt a surge of happiness. He had solved his grandfather's mystery!

"'Famely es the most emportant theng,'" Troy's dad read out loud, and then asked, "What does it mean?"

"Replace some of the *E*'s with *I*'s," Troy explained. "It says, 'Family is the most important thing.'" Troy let the words sink in and then said, "Et's true!"

Mr. Brandt laughed. And Mom and Dad gave Troy a happy hug.

Troy wondered if somewhere his grandfather was smiling, too.

School of Crime

Reading, Writing…and Robbery!

Background Building

This story deals with three friends who all meet as "new kids" on the first day of sixth grade. Being the new kid can be tricky, and it's an experience many students are familiar with. To help set the tone for the story, ask volunteers to talk about times when they were new to something. Broaden the discussion to include what it means to be the new kid on a team, in an organization, or in a family. Were there times when students felt confused or upset? How did they cope with these experiences? Ask students to keep this discussion in mind while they read the mystery.

Focus of Reading Strategy: Summarizing

Remind students that good readers are able to recall important events in a story and retell that story in a condensed way. To help them think about summarizing, have students write down eight to ten significant events in the story as they read.

After Reading

Talk About It

This mystery is told from Franklin's perspective. But Franklin is actually the one who took the book and got his friends in trouble. Discuss what it means to a story when the main character or narrator has some kind of flaw. Do students think this makes the story more interesting and the character more real? Or should the character be 100 percent likable for the story to be good?

Write About It

Ask students to create a journal entry as if they were Michael or Ted writing immediately after they left the library. Have students describe what happened in the library, how they feel about being tricked by Franklin, and what they think the future holds for the three friends.

Vocabulary

Here's a list of words your students will come across in this mystery—as well as their definitions:

accused	claimed a person has done something wrong
cohorts	companions
conspiratorial	indicating involvement in a secret agreement
detention	punishment at school
doodled	drew absentmindedly
frustration	feeling of exasperation
furiously	with anger
racket	a disturbing noise
shelled out	paid
shushed	quieted
Three Musketeers	three close-knit friends in a book by Alexandre Dumas
tolerate	put up with

Reading, Writing... and Robbery!

To solve this sneaky mystery, it will take a careful reader with sharp detective skills.

"Knock it off, you guys!" Franklin shouted at his friends. The other kids in the library jerked up their heads from their books in surprise. And Mrs. Lambeer, the librarian, raised a finger to her lips and shushed him.

"Please, Franklin!" she hissed from her desk across the room. "You and your cohorts need to keep it down!"

Normally, Mrs. Lambeer would kick people out for making such a racket. But the librarian knew why Franklin needed to talk with his friends, and she liked him. Franklin sometimes helped out around the library, like sorting library check-out slips or watching over things when she ran to the teachers' lounge for a cup of coffee. A month ago, he even left the library to grab a piece of chocolate cake from the cafeteria for her.

Mrs. Lambeer definitely had a soft spot for Franklin. But he knew she wouldn't tolerate any more yelling. He also knew it was going to be hard to keep his cool. His two best friends were making him crazy. Right now, Michael and Ted sat on either side of Franklin at the small library table, glaring furiously at each other.

To calm himself down, Franklin nervously doodled his name in his notebook, making a football-shaped circle for the dot over the *i* like he always did.

Franklin remembered the first day of sixth grade, four months ago. He, Michael, and Ted had all been new to the school, and they became instant pals. Over the next few months, they'd spent so much time together that their English teacher called them the "Three Musketeers."

Sure, there had been times, especially about a month ago, when Michael and Ted would hang out or go to see a baseball game without Franklin. And Franklin admitted to himself that he'd felt left out.

Even with the not-so-great memories, he had come to think of the beginning of the year as the good old days. Especially compared to now. For the past month, Michael and Ted hadn't spoken a word to each other. In fact, they did everything they could not to be in the same room. What had happened to Ted and Michael's friendship?

Franklin ran through the events in his head. A month ago, Mrs. Lambeer had accused Michael of checking out a library book and not returning it. He denied borrowing the book. But Mrs. Lambeer said she had the check-out slip with Michael's signature. She insisted he pay the fine plus the cost of the missing book. Michael didn't have a choice and shelled out the cash.

The day after Michael paid for the book, Ted was opening his school locker as Mrs. Lambeer walked by. Just then, the missing book tumbled out of Ted's locker, right at Mrs. Lambeer's feet. She was shocked. She thought Ted must have checked out the book under Michael's name and hidden it in his locker—all to get Michael in trouble. She made Ted write a 500-word essay every day for two weeks about how sorry he was.

So, both Michael and Ted had been punished for something they said they hadn't done. And they both blamed each other. Michael said Ted had checked out the book under his name. Ted said Michael had hidden the book in his locker to frame him. Soon they wouldn't even talk to each other, let alone hang out together.

At first, Franklin thought it was fun to have one-on-one time with each of his pals. He was never lonely and always busy, heading off to see either Ted or Michael. But it was kind of sad spending time with just one of them all the

Comprehension Cliffhangers: Mysteries © 2010 by Bill Doyle, Scholastic Inc.

time. And when Franklin was with either of them, all they did was complain about the other.

Franklin couldn't stand it anymore.

That was why he had told Michael and Ted to meet him here in the library. It seemed like the perfect place to sort everything out and finally reveal who the real crook was.

But they weren't going to get far if Michael and Ted didn't stop throwing daggers at each other with their eyes.

"What's he doing here, Franklin?" Michael demanded, jerking a thumb at Ted.

Franklin sighed in frustration. "Ted has got to be here," he said. "We're going to solve the mystery of the missing book once and for all—"

"What's there to solve?" Michael interrupted. "Ted checked out the book under my name and then kept it in his locker. I got punished for something I didn't do."

"Huh?" Ted said, pretending to swat at flies in the air around him. "Do you hear something, Franklin? Sounds like an annoying bug buzzing around."

"Ted, knock it off," Franklin said, tired of his friends arguing. "You guys, listen—"

"How many times do I have to say it?" Ted threw up his hands. "I didn't take the dumb book. Michael checked it out and put it in my locker. The library card has his name on it. He framed me!"

They were getting really loud. Mrs. Lambeer was busy helping a student, but soon she would notice how much noise they were making. Franklin needed to wrap this up.

"Let's solve the mystery," he said. "What do you remember about that day a month ago, Ted?"

"Why do we need to go over it again?" Ted said. Then he took a breath. "Fine. I was opening my locker, when I noticed there was chocolate or something on the door. I jerked my hand back, and the book fell out. Mrs. Lambeer was going by and saw the book. I got in trouble, and I didn't even do anything."

"Okay," Franklin said. "Why would Michael—or someone you know—put the book in your locker?"

"I don't know," Ted said with a shrug. "Why does Michael think I'd hide a book in my locker to get him in trouble?"

"This is stupid, and it isn't solving anything," Michael said. "I'm out of here."

He started to get up, and Franklin reached out to stop him. "Hold on, there's one piece of evidence that I kept. It might help you guys crack the case. I spoke to Mrs. Lambeer about it this morning." He pushed the library check-out slip toward them. "What do you see?"

Leaning closer to get a better look, Ted said, "It's the library check-out slip for the book that went missing."

Michael pulled the slip toward him and examined it. "That's not even close to my signature. I don't make my M's like that. And what's with that dot on the *i*?"

After a pause, Franklin said, "It looks like a football, doesn't it?"

"Yeah, I guess," Michael said, still gazing at the slip. "What does it mean?"

They're not getting it, Franklin thought. But then Ted sat bolt upright as if someone had whapped him on the head.

"I know!" Ted said. "Oh, man, I get it now. I know who checked out the book and put it in my locker!"

"Who?" Michael asked, talking to Ted directly for the first time in a month. "Who? Tell me!"

Stop Here! Discussion Questions

1. When did Franklin meet Ted and Michael? When did they become friends? Early on, what was their friendship like? Were there any problems?

2. What does Franklin do around the library? Why does Mrs. Lambeer, the librarian, like Franklin so much?

3. Why are Ted and Michael angry with each other? Why does each blame the other for getting in trouble?

4. When they say they are innocent, do you think both Michael and Ted are telling the truth? Could there be another suspect who had something to do with the missing book? Who could it be, and why would that person make a good suspect?

 Now keep reading to see if your predictions are correct.

"I did it."

The words hung in the air. And Franklin still couldn't believe that he was the one who said them.

"What?" Michael said, stunned. He and Ted gazed at Franklin with wide, disbelieving eyes.

"I did it," Franklin repeated, this time louder and with more confidence.

"That dot above the *i* of the signature is shaped like a football. Just like I always dot my *i*'s."

Shaking his head like he couldn't believe his ears, Ted asked, "But why would you do it?"

Franklin was surprised that his friends didn't seem mad, just confused.

"It's stupid," Franklin finally said. "And I don't know if you guys will ever trust me again. The truth is that I was jealous."

"Jealous?" Michael echoed.

Tapping his pencil nervously, Franklin explained, "You guys were starting to hang out without me. You would go to games or movies and not invite me. I wanted to find a way to get you two in a fight. That way, I would be able to spend more time with you."

"That's nuts!" Ted said, and Michael asked, "How did you make it all happen?"

Franklin explained, "Because I help out around the library, I have access to the books and check-out slips. I copied your signature, Michael, onto the check-out slip. Only I made a mistake in dotting the *i*. And then I put the book in your locker, Ted. But that's when I made another mistake. I was also carrying a piece of cake for Mrs. Lambeer, and some of the chocolate got on the handle."

"So that's where that came from!" Ted cried. Luckily, Mrs. Lambeer was still distracted and didn't notice.

"I'm sorry about that," Franklin said, not daring to look his friends in the eye. "I'm sorry about all of it. Really. I was stupid."

"You're right, that was stupid," Michael said.

"Really stupid," Ted agreed. After a second, he added, "But understandable. When it comes to friendships, things can get a little tricky."

"Yeah, and we should know," Michael said and shared a look with Ted.

There was a long silence. Finally, Ted said, "Maybe we could all hang out this weekend."

"I can't," Franklin said miserably.

"Come on, this is dumb," Ted said. "We're all friends. Let's just put this behind us."

"No, I really can't," Franklin said. "I told Mrs. Lambeer what I did this morning. So I'm going to get twice the punishment you guys got. Plus, I have detention the next three Saturdays."

"Oh, well," Ted said. "Going to the movie won't be the same without you, Franklin." He shot Michael a conspiratorial glance.

"Yeah," Michael smiled. "So we'll wait until Sunday."

School of Crime

Chalk It Up to Trouble

Before Reading

Background Building

Much of the tension in this story is caused by an acceptance speech. Ask students if they have heard an acceptance speech. What was the occasion? (*The Oscars, graduation ceremony, athletic banquet, etc.*) Discuss the elements of a strong acceptance speech. Possible answers include: introduction, anecdote or joke, expressions of gratitude, and conclusion. List these elements on the board.

Focus of Reading Strategy: Understanding Cause and Effect

Remind students that a cause is an action, event, person, or thing that makes something happen. What happens as a result is an effect. Go through several examples, such as sunshine on an ice cube and running out of gas while driving. (The sunshine causes the effect of the ice melting, and running out of gas causes the effect of the car stopping.) Ask students to keep an eye out for the cause they think has the greatest effect in this mystery.

After Reading

Talk About It

Mr. Newton was nervous about giving his acceptance speech. He never stated exactly why in the story. Discuss with students why they think he was so anxious. Ask them to look for clues in the text and use their own experiences to make an informed guess, or inference.

Write About It

Return to the list of elements of an acceptance speech that you wrote on the board. Explain to students that they are going to pretend to be speechwriters. Ask them to write the speech for Mr. Newton and try to include all the parts that are listed on the board. Ask for volunteers to read their speeches.

Vocabulary

Here's a list of words your students will come across in this mystery—as well as their definitions:

accordion	musical instrument with a midsection that expands and contracts
annual	happening once a year
bloodshot	inflamed and red
declamations	speeches or presentations
dismiss	give permission to leave
distracted	showing a lack of focus
elocution	expert way of speaking
gravelly	deep and rough-sounding
investigation	examination
motioning	indicating
procedure	way of doing something
rehearsed	practiced
screeching	high-pitched and irritating

Chalk It Up to Trouble

Alice's favorite teacher has just won a big award—but he's gone missing! Can Alice follow the clues and track him down in time?

On Friday afternoon, there wasn't an empty seat to be found in the Hanson Middle School auditorium, and the air was buzzing with excitement. Teachers, students, and families had packed into row after row for the annual Teacher of the Year Award.

Looking his best in a new blue suit, Principal Brewer strode across the stage and spoke into the microphone. "Welcome to the end of a big day!" he announced in his deep, gravelly voice. "We'll invite our Teacher of the Year, Mr. Newton, to the stage in exactly ten minutes to accept his award and say a few words. But before we do that, we've asked fifth grader Gregory Nixon to

Comprehension Cliffhangers: Mysteries © 2010 by Bill Doyle, Scholastic Inc.

play his accordion for us!"

Sitting in the crowd toward the back of the auditorium, Alice Mangan felt her heart start pounding. Not at the thought of having to listen to the accordion, but because she was one of Mr. Newton's sixth-grade students. He really was the best teacher she had ever had, and he definitely deserved the award. She was excited to hear his acceptance speech.

Quickly scanning the crowd, Alice looked around for the bald head of Mr. Newton. It took only a few seconds to figure out that he wasn't in the auditorium.

Where could he be?

Principal Brewer wasn't a patient guy. If Mr. Newton wasn't here in ten minutes when he was called to the stage, Principal Brewer would dismiss the students. Mr. Newton would miss the chance to accept the award in front of the crowd and give his speech.

"Something's wrong," Alice whispered urgently to her best friend, Hank Varick, who was sitting next to her.

"No kidding," Hank agreed. "Gregory Nixon lives next door to me. He just started playing the accordion last week. When I heard him practicing last night, I actually thought it was three angry, howling cats stuck in a bag."

"Hank!" Alice hissed. "This is serious. Mr. Newton isn't here. He's going to miss getting the award and giving his speech. We have to find him. Come on."

She tugged Hank's arm until he followed her. Obviously, students weren't allowed to leave the auditorium during a presentation without permission. So, being careful not to be spotted, the kids crept up the aisle along the wall.

But they didn't need to worry about being seen. The teachers were too distracted by the screeching, whistling, and whining that was coming from Gregory's accordion up on stage to notice them. Unseen, Hank and Alice pushed open the exit. They hurried out of the auditorium into the hallway where...

Tim Privet, the student hallway monitor, had just walked by! He was heading away from them and about to turn the corner at the end of the hallway. But he was only a few feet away!

Alice sucked in a panicked breath. Tim was a seventh grader who took his hallway monitor duties very seriously. If he caught Alice and Hank sneaking out of the auditorium, he would turn them in. They would get detention for sure and end up clapping dirty erasers or sweeping out the cafeteria.

To avoid being spotted, Alice tried to back up into the auditorium. But Hank was right behind her. He slammed into Alice, pushing her forward.

"Ack!" Alice cried, stumbling forward across the hall and crashing into a pile of books that had been stacked outside the library. She went sprawling, scattering two of the books, called *Elegant Elocution* and *Delivering Delightful Declamations*.

Comprehension Cliffhangers: Mysteries © 2010 by Bill Doyle, Scholastic Inc.

Even as she skidded into the locked library door, she wondered: Why had someone left the books here? Why didn't that person just slide them through the return slot?

Alice had bigger problems than worrying about proper library procedure. She thought Tim *must* have heard all the noise she'd just made. He would turn around and see them!

She jumped to her feet, grabbed Hank's arm again, and pulled him into the nearby stairwell to hide. They waited, expecting Tim to burst in right behind them. But the seconds ticked by, and nothing happened. That's when Hank started coughing.

When Alice shot him a warning look, he choked, "Sorry! It's dusty in here!"

It was true. Blue chalk dust floated in the air. The kids who had detention before the assembly must have been clapping erasers in the stairwell, instead of going outside.

"Why didn't Tim chase us in here?" Alice wondered out loud. After a few more seconds, she dared to poke her head out of the stairwell to find out.

There was Tim. But his back was still to them as he turned the corner and headed off to another part of the school. He had not even heard Alice's wipeout, and now she knew why. Tim had headphones clamped to his ears. She could hear the tinny sounds of rock music pumping out of them. She doubted he would hear a stampede race down the hall.

Breathing a sigh of relief, Alice said, "That was close." She looked at her watch. They had only eight minutes to track down Mr. Newton and get him onstage.

"We should check his classroom first," Alice said. Hank nodded, and they left the stairwell, creeping past a nearby mop closet. Alice noticed blue chalk dust on the closet's doorknob as she led the way to Mr. Newton's classroom. When they got there, they found it was empty. Their teacher was nowhere to be seen.

"You're making this into some kind of big mystery," Hank said, a little out of breath from all the running around. "What does it matter if Mr. Newton misses the ceremony? They'll still give him the Teacher of the Year Award."

"It matters!" Alice insisted. Yesterday she had walked into the classroom and found Mr. Newton practicing his acceptance speech. He seemed really nervous as he rehearsed in front of a small mirror. It was obviously an important speech to him, and she didn't want him to be disappointed.

But she didn't tell Hank all of that. Instead, she said, "There must be a clue to where he is somewhere in this classroom," she said. "We just have to find it."

Glancing around, Hank asked, "Do you think he got sick from using the wrong chalk?"

Everyone in school knew that Mr. Newton had to use a special kind of chalk. He was allergic to regular chalk. It made his eyes turn red and his face puff up.

"No," Alice said, taking a look at the yellow chalk sitting in the chalkboard railing. "This is the special kind he uses."

"Here's something," Hank called, tapping a notebook on the teacher's desk. "He was taking notes about giving speeches. It's a bunch of quotes from books about how to impress people when speaking in public."

Alice knew they shouldn't be reading Mr. Newton's notebook. But it was wide open, and it was for a good cause. Next to the notebook was Mr. Newton's calendar. For today's date, he'd written a list of things to do:

Give history test
Return books to the library
Accept award and give speech

As Alice finished reading, Hank was tapping his watch. "There's only five minutes left!" he said. Alice could tell he was into the investigation now.

Alice was running through the clues in her head: the names of the library books she had tripped over, the blue chalk dust in the stairwell, and the quotations in the notebook. She had the answer!

"What should we do?" Hank asked impatiently.

"Let's go get Mr. Newton," she said.

Before Hank could ask any questions, Alice hurried out of the classroom, motioning for him to follow. This time, when they entered the hall, they weren't as lucky. Tim Privet was at the end of the hall, but this time he was facing them. He took off his headphones and shouted, "Halt!"

"Halt?" Hank whispered, rolling his eyes. Alice had to agree. Tim was being a little dramatic. For the third time, she grabbed Hank's arm and pulled him down the hallway away from Tim.

"Alice!" Hank shouted. "Where are we going?"

"Right here," she answered, stopping in front of the mop closet they had passed earlier, next to the stairwell. As Tim raced down the hall after them, Alice knocked on the closet door. It creaked open like the lid of a coffin in a horror movie.

Hank was shocked to see two bloodshot eyes framed by a blue face peering out at them.

Alice, on the other hand, looked completely relieved.

Comprehension Cliffhangers: Mysteries © 2010 by Bill Doyle, Scholastic Inc.

Stop Here! **Discussion Questions**

1. Why does Alice want to find Mr. Newton so badly? What are a few obstacles that might keep her from tracking him down?

2. Alice lists clues, like the library books. Take a look at the titles of the books. What do you think they're about? Why would they be important to solving the case?

3. Another clue Alice lists is chalk dust. Where has she seen chalk dust during this story? Does that help you solve the mystery of the missing teacher?

4. Who do you think is in the mop closet? Why would Alice be relieved to see that person?

 Now keep reading to see if your predictions are on target.

"Come on out, Mr. Newton," Alice said to the figure in the doorway. And Hank was even more shocked than before to see she was right. It was Mr. Newton!

By now, Tim had caught up with them. "You two are in big trouble," he announced, pointing at Alice and Hank.

But Mr. Newton held up his hand. "It's okay, Tim. Alice and Hank are with me."

Tim turned toward Mr. Newton, his eyes widening when he saw the red eyes and slightly blue face. "Who are...?" Then he recognized the teacher. "Oh, sure thing, Mr. Newton. Sorry."

After Tim had wandered off down the hall, Mr. Newton asked, "How did you find me?"

"I have no idea," Hank said, looking at Alice for an explanation.

"I followed the clues," she said to Mr. Newton. "On your calendar, we saw that you planned to return the library books on your way to give your speech. But, I think, as you were about to slide them through the return slot, you must have heard Tim coming down the hall."

Mr. Newton nodded. "That's true. I heard the music coming through his headphones."

Comprehension Cliffhangers: Mysteries © 2010 by Bill Doyle, Scholastic Inc.

"So," Alice continued, "you just left the books in front of the library door and ducked into the stairwell like we did."

"But why?" Hank asked. "You're a teacher, Mr. Newton! Why would you care if Tim Privet saw you returning a bunch of books?"

Alice knew, but she waited for Mr. Newton to explain. "I was embarrassed," he said. "I had borrowed books about giving speeches. I felt silly and didn't want people to think they were giving the award to the wrong guy. You know, to someone who couldn't even speak in public. But once I was in the stairwell with all that blue chalk dust, I felt even worse."

"The dust from the kids clapping erasers got all over you and made your eyes red and puffy," Alice said. As she spoke, she went into the mop closet. After soaking a paper towel in water from the sink, she handed it to Mr. Newton.

"Thanks," he said, running the cool cloth over his face and eyes. "I had to get out of the stairwell, so I ducked down the hall to the nearest place to hide, which was in here in the mop closet."

"That's why there was blue chalk dust on the door handle!" Alice said.

Mr. Newton nodded, but he wasn't smiling. He indicated his puffy face. "Now there's no way I can go on stage looking like this."

"Of course you can!" Hank said, and Alice added, "You look better already." He hoped she didn't see her fingers were crossed.

"I don't know . . ." Mr. Newton seemed tempted. From inside the gym, they suddenly heard the sound of applause followed by Principal Brewer thanking Gregory for playing his accordion. They listened as the principal started to introduce Mr. Newton.

"Believe me," Alice said, "if that audience can clap for Gregory Nixon's accordion playing, they're going to love your speech!"

"Good point," Mr. Newton said, laughing. "Okay, let's go! Thanks to you two, I'm ready to accept my award."

Comprehension Cliffhangers: Mysteries © 2010 by Bill Doyle, Scholastic Inc.

School of Crime

A Real Crack in the Case

Before Reading

Background Building

Point out to students that this story is written in the first person. That means, the narrative is told by one character who uses *I* (first-person singular) and *we* (first-person plural). Have students offer examples of books they have read that use this device. Now discuss with students how a first-person perspective might affect a story.

Focus of Reading Strategy:
Understanding Genre—Mystery

"A Real Crack in the Case" is a mystery. Based on their reading so far, discuss with students what elements they can expect to find in this and other mysteries. Possible answers include:

* a crime or wrongdoing of some kind
* a detective (professional or amateur) to solve the case
* suspects or possible wrongdoers
* clues that point the detective in the right direction
* discovery of the truth and a conclusion

After Reading

Talk About It

Point out that characters in this story have drawn conclusions that are not always fair. Ask students why drawing quick conclusions would not be a good idea for a detective. Discuss how this might lead to ignoring important clues and letting the real culprit get away.

Write About It

Roz is an important character in this story. Using the first person, have students rewrite the story from her point of view.

Vocabulary

Here's a list of words your students will come across in this mystery—as well as their definitions:

blazing	intense
clucked	made short clicking sounds
dramatic	larger than life
evaporated	disappeared
flabbergasted	really confused
genuinely	honestly
jarring	startling
reenactment	acting out of a past event
remodeled	changed the structure of something
self-consciously	with uncomfortable feelings of one's own supposed flaws
smattering	small amount
smirked	smiled in a self-satisfied or smug way
spluttered	made a choking sound
wrongly	incorrectly

A Real Crack
in the Case

**Janet's main enemy has been accused of stealing
answers to a test. Will Janet help unravel the mystery,
or let past feelings prevent justice?**

I had just finished the last science test of the year, a few minutes early. Staring out the window, I was thinking about all the things I would be doing that summer. Swimming, reading detective books, playing softball—but mostly, I was excited that I wouldn't have to even see Roz Rosetta for three whole months. At my all-girls school, she was kind of the bully of the sixth grade. You know the type. She was really pushy. And she'd always try to get her way by shouting until you just gave up.

Speaking of shouting, I was still daydreaming when our teacher, Mrs. Foley, rushed into the classroom. While we take tests, she sits in her little office, which is right through a doorway at the front of the classroom. I had been expecting her to tell us the test time was up and that we should put our pencils down. Instead, Mrs. Foley yelled, "The answer sheet has been stolen!"

Mrs. Foley wasn't like Roz. She never even raised her voice. So it was jarring to hear her shout. Plus, she looked frazzled, and there was a spot of something on her sleeve. I'd never seen her so upset.

Pointing her finger straight at Roz, Mrs. Foley said angrily, "You took the answer sheet with all the answers to the test. It was in my office when I first went in there, and now it's gone."

"What?" Roz spluttered. "You think I stole it?"

"It could only have been you," Mrs. Foley said, her eyes blazing. "You got up to go to the bathroom during the test. You must have taken it then."

Now, as you've probably figured out by now, Roz was not my favorite person. But, I had to admit, I didn't think she was the thief. She looked genuinely shocked.

I decided to do my good deed for the day and offer my help. "Let's have a dramatic reenactment," I suggested.

"What's that?" Roz asked. Then, noticing I was the one who had spoken, she added, "Sounds pretty dumb."

I ignored her comment. "Reenactments are big parts of detective work. People act out what they know about a crime, hoping some new fact will come to light," I said. "It's kind of like putting on a play."

Roz smirked. But Mrs. Foley told me, "All right, Janet. We have 15 minutes until the end of the day. You have that long to prove to me that Roz didn't take the answer sheet. If we can't find it, you will all have to retake the test."

The ten other girls in the class groaned.

"And the consequences for Roz will be far worse," Mrs. Foley continued. "She will fail the class and have to take summer school."

This seemed to hit Roz like a ton of bricks. Her smirk disappeared, and she couldn't even speak. I guessed there was a first time for everything. The stakes were very high. But I was up to the challenge.

"Let's go to the scene of the crime," I said.

Mrs. Foley told the other girls to stay in their seats, and she went back to her office with Roz and me. The only furniture in the room was Mrs. Foley's desk and a chair. And there was a hook near the door where the bathroom pass normally hung. That was it.

Everything else had been removed. The office was going to be remodeled over the summer. The workers had already ripped off the baseboards that ran along the bottom of the walls. They were going to knock the center wall down and combine the office with the room next door, which is where our lockers were.

I looked around the nearly empty office. "Okay, let's start the reenactment.

Where was the last place you saw the answer sheet, Mrs. Foley?"

"It was on my desk," she answered.

I put a book on her desk to represent the answer sheet. "And where were you?"

"I was sitting right here." Mrs. Foley took a seat at her desk, sitting upright and facing away from the door. That's when I noticed there was a little pool of liquid on the desk. It matched the liquid on Mrs. Foley's shirt.

I clucked my tongue. "Mrs. Foley, if the reenactment is going to work, you have to do exactly what you were doing at the time the crime took place. You weren't sitting straight up like that. You were napping."

"I was . . . I was resting my eyes!" Mrs. Foley protested. Then, blushing, she admitted, "Okay, I was napping. How did you know, Janet?"

"There's a little drool on the desk and on your shirt," I said. "The kind of drool that comes with napping."

"Yuck," Roz said, and Mrs. Foley shot her a warning look.

Before Roz could get herself in more trouble, I said quickly, "Okay, let's keep going. Mrs. Foley was sitting at her desk with her back to the door and resting her eyes. What were you doing, Roz?"

"This is stupid," Roz said. When I just kept staring at her, waiting for an answer, she finally said, "Fine! In the middle of taking the test, I came into the office to get the bathroom pass."

"Did you leave your locker key on the hook in its place, Roz?" I asked.

"Yes," she snapped.

In the past, girls had forgotten to put the bathroom pass back on the hook after using it. So Mrs. Foley instituted a new rule: When you took the bathroom pass, you had to leave your locker key on the hook in its place. This reminded girls to put the pass back.

"When you were done, did you drop off the bathroom pass and pick up your key?" I asked.

"No," Roz said, reaching into her pocket and taking it out. "The test today really freaked me out. I forgot to put the bathroom key back and pick up my locker key."

Nodding, Mrs. Foley held out Roz's locker key. "That's how I knew it was Roz who was in here. I found her key with her name on it on the hook. She was the only other person in here, so she must have taken the answer sheet." Mrs. Foley started to stand up as if the case had been solved.

"Let's not get ahead of ourselves," I said. "Let's finish with what we know. What did you do right after you took the bathroom key and left your own key in its place, Roz?"

"I opened the door," she said, "and I left."

"Don't just tell me, show me," I said. "This is a dramatic reenactment."

Sighing, Roz opened the door to the office. A slight breeze from the classroom caused the hair on her forehead to blow back. For the first time, I could see that Roz had a smattering of freckles underneath. Freckles were the kinds of things she would make fun of on other kids. She must have worked really hard to hide them. She pushed the hair back into place.

Looking at her freckles, a lightbulb had gone on in my head.

"That's it!" I cried, taking a quick look at the wall that separated the office from the locker room next door.

"What's it?" Mrs. Foley asked.

"I just figured it out!" I said. "Follow me." I led them out the door through the classroom and into the hallway. We walked down the hall and into the locker room, where I took a look around.

"What are the odds?" I wondered out loud, and walked over to Roz's locker. "Roz, can you open your locker?"

Mrs. Foley handed her key back, and Roz crouched to unlock her locker. She swung open the door, and inside, on the floor of the locker . . . was the answer sheet.

"So it was you, Roz!" Mrs. Foley cried. She was furious.

But Roz was even angrier. She wheeled on me. "I thought you were going to help me! I should have known you were going to frame me!"

I held out my hands. "Don't you get it? I just proved you're innocent. You couldn't have possibly taken the answer sheet."

Stop Here! Discussion Questions

1. Who is telling the story? What do you know about her? Does she like Roz? Why do you think the narrator would want to help solve the case?

2. What is missing? Why does Mrs. Foley think that Roz is the one who took it?

3. What is a dramatic reenactment? Who uses reenactments like these? Why do you think they would be useful?

4. What do you think happened to the answer sheet? Do you think Roz took it? How did it end up in her locker?

OKAY! **Now keep reading to see if you cracked the case!**

"What?" Roz looked flabbergasted. "What did you just say?"

I explained calmly, "You put your locker key on the hook before you left Mrs. Foley's office. If you took the answer sheet at that time, you wouldn't have been able to open your locker and put the answer sheet inside."

"That's right!" Roz said. "I didn't have my key."

"So how did the answer sheet get inside her locker?" Mrs. Foley asked.

Glancing at Roz, I said, "The solution is in your freckles."

Roz looked surprised and self-consciously touched her forehead.

"I never noticed you had freckles before," I said. "And I wouldn't have if that little breeze hadn't blown back your hair when you opened the office door. That breeze is the key to everything."

Mrs. Foley started to ask me a question. But I said, "Let's run the reenactment again. It will make sense then."

I led everyone back to the office and closed the door. I asked Mrs. Foley to take a seat and put the answer sheet on her desk. "This time, we'll use the actual answer sheet instead of a book to represent it," I said. "Now, Roz, open the door like you did right after you picked up the bathroom pass."

She opened the door. We watched as the breeze that had blown back Roz's hair lifted the answer sheet off the desk. The page slid across the floor and halfway under the crack in the wall.

"Do you see?" I exclaimed. "The breeze is the thief. Not Roz. It blew the answer sheet off the desk, through the crack in the wall, and right into her locker. Roz didn't notice because she was leaving the room, and Mrs. Foley didn't see it because she was napping."

Mrs. Foley's eyes went from the door to her desk to the crack under the wall. The teacher's anger evaporated. "Oh, my," Mrs. Foley said. "Roz, I am so sorry for wrongly accusing you! I apologize."

Just then, the school bell rang. I had solved the case just in time!

A few minutes later, I had packed my book bag and was heading out the door when I felt a tapping on my shoulder. It was Roz.

"Hey, Janet," she said quietly. "Thanks for helping me." She gave me a smile and a big, friendly hug.

Now it was my turn to be speechless.

Comprehension Cliffhangers: Mysteries © 2010 by Bill Doyle, Scholastic Inc.

Foul Play

Ticket to Danger

Background Building

This mystery takes place in a huge football stadium. Ask students who have attended big football games to describe what they saw, tasted, and even felt inside the stadium. How is being there live different from watching the game at home on TV? Ask why it's important to have the right ticket at the stadium. What might happen if there was some kind of mix-up and students received the wrong ticket?

Focus of Reading Strategy: Making Connections

Skilled readers connect people and events in stories to experiences in their own lives. Students might read about a place or person that reminds them of somewhere they've visited or someone they've met. As they read this story, have students keep an eye out for things that trigger memories of their own experiences at sporting events.

Talk About It

Point out that many coaches communicate directly with players using coded messages or hand signals. Ask students why coaches might worry about other people figuring out what they were saying.

In this story, a coach uses a radio to talk to the quarterback through headphones in the player's helmet. Ask students to imagine other (perhaps more secure) ways that a coach on the sidelines could communicate with players on the field.

Write About It

Point out that T.D. is a sports detective who cracks cases dealing with athletics. Ask students to create an advertisement that would run online or in magazines that would help T.D. bring in new clients. What would make a good slogan for such an ad? Use real ads as examples to help students determine important elements to include.

Vocabulary

Here's a list of words your students will come across in this mystery—as well as their definitions:

absorbed	very focused on something
apparently	seems to be true, but may not be
batter	hit repeatedly
betrayed	deceived by
disguise	attire worn to conceal the wearer's identity
hunch	impression that something might be true
impatiently	in a short-tempered way
initials	first letters of someone's name
moolah	slang for money
narrowed	made less wide
randomly	in a haphazard way
rivals	competing groups
victorious	having won something

Ticket to Danger

Out for a day of watching football, sports detective T.D. stumbles upon his strangest case yet.

The sky was blue. The air was crisp. And the smell of hot dogs and popcorn filled the air. It was a perfect fall afternoon for a football game.

Twelve-year-old T.D. rushed over to the stadium ticket window to pick up his ticket. He had ordered it online and knew it would be waiting for him.

"Name, please?" the lady behind the glass asked. She looked tired and worn out.

"T.D.," he answered.

"No, not your initials," the ticket lady snapped impatiently, glancing at the line of football fans forming behind T.D. The last game of the season was about to start, and no one wanted to miss any of the action between the Jellyfish and the Sharks.

The two teams were bitter rivals on and off the field. The owner of the Sharks

Comprehension Cliffhangers: Mysteries © 2010 by Bill Doyle, Scholastic Inc.

was Thalia Desmond, who couldn't stand the owner of the Jellyfish. She pushed her coaches and players to do whatever it took to win. The Jellyfish, on the other hand, were tired of losing to the Sharks and were determined to be victorious. It promised to be an exciting game.

"What's your *full* name?" the ticket lady was asking. "So I can find your ticket."

"Timothy Davies," T.D. said. "But everyone calls me T.D., you know, like touchdown. Because I'm a sports detective, and I always score 'touchdowns' against the crooks. I just cracked another case, and I'm looking to relax and watch the game today."

The ticket lady held up a hand to get him to stop talking, and said, "TMI."

"Is that *your* name?" T.D. asked, watching her randomly pluck a ticket envelope out of the box in front of her.

"No," she said. "TMI stands for Too Much Information." Sliding the envelope toward him, she waved him aside and shouted past him, "Next in line!"

"Okay, thanks . . . bye," T.D. mumbled and hurried away off to the stadium entrance. Making his way inside, he followed the signs to his section. When he arrived there, however, he knew something was wrong. This wasn't the seat he'd reserved online. The lady had been in such a hurry, she'd given him the wrong ticket.

Oh, well, T.D. thought. With the game about to start, it was too late to go back to the ticket window. And like the ticket he had originally bought, the seat was on the 50-yard line. It was just on the opposite side of the stadium.

T.D. sat down and took out his binoculars. He watched the players warming up, and then lifted the binoculars slightly to see if he could tell who was sitting in the seat he had bought online. He spotted a woman in huge sunglasses and a giant sun hat; she was pushing something that looked like an envelope at the man next to her.

"That's strange," T.D. mumbled to himself.

Before he could figure out what was happening, the referee blew his whistle and the game got under way. Soon, T.D. was totally absorbed in the action, watching the two rival teams run, tackle, and pass up and down the field as they attempted to score.

From his new seat, T.D. had a good view of not only the game, but also of Coach James of the Jellyfish talking into his radio headset. He was calling plays to the Jellyfish quarterback, who had headphones in his helmet tuned to the same channel.

To keep others from overhearing the next play, T.D. knew Coach James had an interesting system. He picked a new channel number for each game, according to the number of pancakes he ate that morning. If he had 18 pancakes at the Pancake House, the channel would be set to 18. Since the number always changed, it would be hard for anyone to figure out the channel and listen in.

T.D. was thinking this was a pretty cool idea when something jabbed him in the ribs. He lowered his binoculars and looked down. A hand was pushing a folded piece of paper at him.

"Here," a raspy voice said. "Take it."

T.D. turned to the seat next to him where a hulking man now sat. The man wore what looked like a restaurant uniform: a bowtie and a white shirt that was stained with syrup.

The big man was trying to get T.D. to take the piece of paper, which T.D. finally did. He unfolded the paper and saw it had the number 21 written on it. "Uh, thanks," T.D. said, not sure what else to say.

"Shhh. Don't talk," the man commanded in a rough voice. "You know the drill. Just hand over the moolah."

"Moolah?" T.D. asked. What was this creepy guy talking about?

"You know, dough, bucks, cashola," the man said. But when T.D. still didn't get it, he blew out air in frustration. "Money! Hand over the money. Good disguise, by the way. No one would ever know that you're a middle-aged woman."

"There's a reason for that," T.D. said. "I'm not a woman. I'm a 12-year-old boy."

T.D. decided it was time to stop talking to this weird man. Lifting his binoculars, he went back to checking out the crowd. In a moment of surprise, T.D. saw that the woman sitting in his original seat across the stadium was now looking directly at him through her own binoculars. He watched as she slapped her forehead, as if she'd just realized a mistake. Then she got up from her seat and headed toward T.D.

Meanwhile, the big guy next to T.D. was getting even stranger. "Stop being funny and hand over the money," the man growled. Cracking his knuckles, he leaned closer to T.D. "I don't want to get rough."

T.D. nodded. "Good. I don't want that either."

"Well, you don't always get what you want," the man said and stood up. "Come with me."

The man reached out to grab T.D.'s arm. People around were shouting like crazy as a player ran down the field. No one would hear T.D. yelling for help.

Just then, the woman from across the stadium arrived. "What are you doing over here?" she demanded of the man. Then she turned to T.D. "You're in my seat, kid. Beat it."

She snatched the piece of paper out of T.D.'s hand and waved him away. Eager to get away from these two, T.D. headed down the steps to the sidelines and stopped. He needed to think for a second. What was going on?

Looking for answers, he glanced back up at the man and the woman. She now had a walkie-talkie in her hand and was speaking into it. T.D. couldn't hear what she was saying, but he could see she was looking at the number on the paper.

T.D. had planned to take a break from mysteries today, but apparently he was

Comprehension Cliffhangers: Mysteries © 2010 by Bill Doyle, Scholastic Inc.

in the middle of one. So, as with any case, he thought about the clues.

Clue #1: The big man with syrup on his uniform had tried to make T.D. pay for a piece of paper with a number on it.

Clue #2: The woman with sunglasses and the sun hat was obviously in disguise. Who was she?

Acting on a hunch, T.D. reached into his pocket and took out the envelope the ticket lady had given him. He read the name on the envelope. This was the name of the woman who had ended up with his seat. The initials were the same as his, but the full name was different.

Seeing the name, T.D. suddenly knew exactly what was going on. He had to get to Coach James! He rushed along the sidelines until he reached the Jellyfish's benches.

"Coach James!" he shouted, trying to get the coach's attention.

But the coach just ignored him and kept calling the next play into his radio headset. T.D. had no choice. Pushing past the players, he reached up, grabbed the headset off the coach's head and threw it on the ground.

The entire team rumbled to their feet and surrounded T.D. Coach James looked furious. "You've got some explaining to do!"

Stop Here! Discussion Questions

1. What are the names of the teams playing in today's game? Do the two teams like each other? Who is Thalia Desmond? Who is Coach James?

2. Who is T.D.? Why do people call him just by his initials? Why is he at the game today?

3. Where does T.D. sit? Is it the same seat that he reserved online? Where is the seat he originally bought?

4. What do you know about the creepy man who sits next to T.D.? What is he wearing? What stains are on his shirt? Do you think these stains might be important?

5. Can you guess the identity of the woman in disguise?

OKAY! Now keep reading to see if you cracked the case!

"Call a time-out, Coach," T.D. said. "You're being tricked."

Coach James's eyes narrowed. But something about T.D.'s tone must have convinced him to listen. He made a hand signal, calling for a time-out.

"Okay, you've got one minute," Coach James said, turning back to T.D.

He took a deep breath and announced, "You've been betrayed by your pancakes." Seeing the coach's blank expression, he decided to start over. "I was given the wrong ticket and sat in the wrong seat."

Coach James tapped his watch. Time was running out. "So? Complain to the ticket window."

"I was given Thalia Desmond's seat. As you know, she's the owner of the Sharks." T.D. held up the empty ticket envelope with Thalia Desmond's name on it. "We both have the same initials. Thalia Desmond was supposed to sit next to the waiter from the restaurant where you had breakfast. He knows how many pancakes you ate this morning. It was 21, right?"

Coach James gave a surprised start and then nodded. Now, he was really interested. "Go on."

"Since I had the wrong ticket, I ended up sitting next to the waiter," T.D. said. "Because he knows the number of pancakes you ate, the waiter knows which radio channel you use to talk to your quarterback. He sold that information to Thalia Desmond so she could listen in. She'll know which plays you call!"

Coach James just stared at T.D., and T.D. couldn't tell what he was thinking.

Just then, the referee blew his whistle. The time-out was over. It was time to get playing again.

"What are you going to do, Coach?" T.D. asked.

"Finish the game," Coach James said. "I'll tell my quarterback to switch channels again. We'll beat the Sharks fair and square, and then I'll let the officials know what Thalia's been up to." He patted T.D.'s shoulder. "Good work, kid."

"Thanks, Coach," T.D. said. "I'm just glad I could score another touchdown for justice!"

Comprehension Cliffhangers: Mysteries © 2010 by Bill Doyle, Scholastic Inc.

Foul Play

To Catch a Catching Thief

Before Reading

Background Building

A collector's item is at the center of this mystery. Ask students what a collector does. *(Simply put, he or she collects items that are the same kind of thing, such as stamps, matchbooks, cars, boats, pens, ties—anything!)* Discuss with students why people might enjoy collecting. What makes it a fun and rewarding hobby? What makes an item, such as a baseball caught by a fan at an important game, suddenly more valuable than other similar items?

Focus of Reading Strategy:
Visualizing

Visualizing is a way of forming mental pictures. Good readers "see" the action in their minds as they read. While they are reading, ask students to visualize the scene where T.D. uses the 3-D viewing room.

After Reading

Talk About It

Ask students: Why did Mrs. Simmons hide the fact that she still had the baseball? What were her motives? Why did she want to keep it? What about the way the character was set up makes this a surprise?

Write About It

Ask students to take another look at the scene where Mr. Brevin introduces T.D. to the 3-D viewing room and the holograms. Have students write down different things they learn about the room from this scene. Now have them create how-to guides or manuals about how to use the viewing rooms for people who have just bought such a device.

Vocabulary

Here's a list of words your students will come across in this mystery—as well as their definitions:

3-D	having a three-dimensional appearance
choked up	emotional
collectors	people who collect things of a specific type
conference	meeting
defiant	boldly resisting authority
disguised	dressed to change one's appearance
donation	gift, usually money, given to a charity
exhilarating	lively, refreshing
handkerchief	cloth used to wipe areas of the face
holograms	three-dimensional photographic images
orphanage	a home for children who have lost their parents
plush	luxurious

To Catch a Catching Thief

T.D. enters a high-tech room straight out of science fiction to discover who stole a baseball from an old woman.

With a *ding!* the elevator doors slid open, and T.D., the famous 12-year-old sports detective, stepped out. He found himself six stories beneath the stadium, in the plush offices of Mr. Brevin, the owner of the Whiskers baseball team. The offices were deep underground, but a gorgeous flower display on a table covered with a green cloth made the place feel comfortable.

Mr. Brevin, a white-haired man with a constant frown, was waiting for him. "T.D., glad you could come down so quickly."

"Happy to help out if I can," T.D. said. "What's going on?"

"It's about something that happened at today's game," Mr. Brevin said. As always, he was all business and got right to the point. "You probably know that one of my players, Davy Crushlink, set the record for hitting more home runs than any other batter in the history of Whiskers Stadium."

"Sure, I heard he hit it into the stands, and some lucky fan caught it," T.D. said. "That ball will be worth a lot of money to collectors."

"Exactly," Mr. Brevin said. "And that's why you're here. Someone stole the ball from the old lady who caught it."

"So you want me to help you track down the thief? I'm going to need more details about what happened."

"Come with me," Mr. Brevin instructed, and they went into a small office where three people were sitting in different corners of the room. One was an older woman with silver hair. Mr. Brevin led T.D. over and introduced her. "T.D., this is Mrs. Simmons, who runs an orphanage in town. She's the lucky fan who caught the ball that broke the home-run record."

Mrs. Simmons sniffed and dabbed her eyes with a handkerchief. "I *was* the one who caught the ball, but I don't know how lucky I am. Just after the ball landed in my hands, someone disguised in a green hood and clothes ran up to me, snatched the ball away, and then took off!"

The old woman suddenly got more choked up. "I always told everyone," she continued with tears running down her cheeks, "that if ever I found anything valuable, I would sell it to make money for the orphans in my care. And now, what will I tell my little angels?"

Mrs. Simmons got so upset she had to leave the room to get a glass of water in the lobby. Once she was gone, Mr. Brevin said, "Now I'll introduce you to our two witnesses."

He led T.D. over to a kid dressed in a hot dog vendor's uniform. His name was Nathan, and he looked to be about 18. When T.D. asked him if he saw the thief dressed in green, Nathan shook his head. "No," he said. "I was just leaving the section to pick up more hot dogs to sell. In fact, I have to get back to my box of buns. I left them out in the lobby."

After Nathan had left, Mr. Brevin and T.D. turned to the last person in the room. This was Mr. Garton, a businessman from out of town.

"Before you ask, I can't tell you anything new," Mr. Garton said. "I know you think I'm a suspect. But I wasn't even supposed to be at the game. I was supposed to be at a work conference. When I saw the cameras following the ball to the old lady, I ducked under a seat, out of sight, so my boss wouldn't see me at the game. I didn't see the thief. Can I go out to the lobby now? I need to make a phone call."

"You can go," Mr. Brevin told him, waving toward the door.

"Not much to go on," T.D. said, now that he was alone with Mr. Brevin in the room. "Were there any other witnesses at the scene? Anyone else who might have seen the thief steal the ball?"

Comprehension Cliffhangers: Mysteries © 2010 by Bill Doyle, Scholastic Inc.

Mr. Brevin shook his head. "Crushlink never hit home runs into left field like he did today. So everyone was jammed over in right field, waiting to catch the ball there."

"What about the cameras the businessman mentioned?" T.D. said. "Is there a video recording of the game?"

Chuckling, Mr. Brevin said, "Oh, we can do better than that."

Mr. Brevin opened a door and showed T.D. into a completely bare room without a single piece of furniture. The walls, floor, and ceiling were all bright white.

"This is our 3-D viewing room," Mr. Brevin said. "We're developing one for every home. You watch from the middle of the room, and it makes you feel like you're actually at the game. You can tell the computer to freeze the image or go back. Watch this." Mr. Brevin spoke a little more loudly, "Computer, play the sequence with Mrs. Simmons catching the ball."

There was a blip of light, and then the whole room was bursting with color. Figures and shapes popped out of thin air. T.D. suddenly felt like he was in the stands of the stadium's left field. Mrs. Simmons was there, and so were the hot dog vendor and the businessman. Everything looked real, but when T.D. put out his hand to touch a seat, his hand went right through it.

"They're just holograms," Mr. Brevin said. "You know, 3-D images created by a computer. They look real, but they're just pictures. It's like standing in the middle of an instant replay. Keep your eye on the action."

T.D. watched the recorded scene play out, and it was just as he had imagined. The hot dog vendor was leaving the section and had his back to Mrs. Simmons. The businessman was diving to the ground to avoid being seen by the cameras. And Mrs. Simmons was jumping to her feet, her hands extended to catch the ball.

And the second she did, a figure dressed in green raced down her row in three quick steps, pushed into her, and kept running.

"Freeze!" Mr. Brevin said. All the action stopped. "Any ideas, T.D.?"

"Not yet," T.D. said. "I better see that again."

"Computer, replay that last scene," Mr. Brevin said.

There was a blip of light, and the action started again from the point just before Mrs. Simmons caught the ball. Once again, the hot dog vendor was leaving the section, the businessman was dropping to the ground, and Mrs. Simmons was jumping to her feet. As before, the second she caught the ball, a figure in green raced toward her. In four steps, the person reached her, pushed past her, and kept running.

"Freeze," T.D. said, and then added, "I need to see it just one more time."

Impatient for answers, Mr. Brevin sighed, but said, "Computer, replay scene."

With a bright blip of light, the action started again at the beginning. But this time, just as the thief in green got close to Mrs. Simmons, T.D. shouted "Freeze!" And the image went still.

Comprehension Cliffhangers: Mysteries © 2010 by Bill Doyle, Scholastic Inc.

"What do you see?" Mr. Brevin said.

"I think you'd be surprised how real one of these people actually is," T.D. said.

Shaking his head, Mr. Brevin said, "I told you. These are just holograms. Nothing is real here."

"Oh, yes, there is," T.D. said. And to prove it, he took Mr. Brevin's hand and put it on the shoulder of the green crook.

Mr. Brevin let out a little cry and jerked his hand back.

"That's not a hologram!" he gasped in surprise. "That's a real person!"

Stop Here! Discussion Questions

1. Why has Mr. Brevin asked T.D. to come to see him? Where are his offices?

2. Why is Mrs. Simmons so upset? What did she plan on doing with the money she might have raised by selling the ball?

3. Who does Mr. Brevin think the thief might be? Where were the two witnesses when the crime took place?

4. What is the "3-D viewing room"? What is a hologram? Why would a room like this be useful to a detective like T.D.?

5. Can you guess the identity of the "real person" who Mr. Brevin touches?

OKAY! **Now keep reading to see if you solved the case!**

Mr. Brevin ordered the computer to power down, and the holograms disappeared. Now only Mr. Brevin, T.D., and thief in green remained. Mr. Brevin reached over and removed the thief's green hood. T.D. wasn't surprised by the identity of the crook.

Mr. Brevin was, however, and shouted, "Mrs. Simmons!"

T.D. was used to crooks turning angry and defiant when they were caught. Instead, Mrs. Simmons's shoulders slumped, and tears sprang from her eyes.

"I'm sorry!" Mrs. Simmons sobbed.

Turning to T.D., Mr. Brevin said, "I don't get it. Why is Mrs. Simmons dressed up like the thief?"

T.D. handed Mrs. Simmons a fresh handkerchief. "There is no thief, Mr. Brevin. She made up the story about the man dressed in green who stole the baseball. When she found out we would be watching the replay of what happened in here, she knew we wouldn't see the man in green because he doesn't exist. The only way she wouldn't get caught in a lie would be to dress up as the imaginary thief and pretend to be a hologram in the scene."

Still looking shocked, Mr. Brevin asked, "Where would she get the costume?"

"I bet if you check your lobby display of flowers, you'll see the green cloth is gone," T.D. said. "Mrs. Simmons turned it into the disguise."

Mr. Brevin gazed at Mrs. Simmons. "But why?"

"I couldn't help myself!" Mrs. Simmons wailed. "When I caught the ball today, it was the most exhilarating thing that's ever happened to me. It sounds awful, but I didn't want to sell the ball to raise money for the orphanage. I do everything for those children. I just wanted to hold onto something for myself."

"Why didn't you just keep it?" T.D. asked.

"I always promised that I would sell it. I didn't want people to think I was selfish." Mrs. Simmons blew her nose, then asked, "How did you know it was me?"

"The first time we watched the action," T.D. said, "you took three steps to reach the hologram of yourself. The second time, you took four steps. Since we were watching a recording, the steps should have been the same both times."

As Mrs. Simmons nodded, Mr. Brevin asked, "Where is the ball?"

"It's right here," Mrs. Simmons said, reaching under the green cloth she still wore and into her purse. She held the ball out to the owner. "I'm sorry."

T.D. felt bad for her. He knew it was simple to get caught up in the excitement of sports. He was a sports detective, after all. Mrs. Simmons had made a mistake, but he didn't think she should be punished.

Mr. Brevin must have agreed, because he refused to take the ball from her. "No, keep it," he said. "I'll make a donation to the orphanage. That way, you can hold onto the ball, and the children still get the money."

Seeing Mrs. Simmons's new tears—ones of joy—T.D. said, "Now that sounds like a real home run!"

Comprehension Cliffhangers: Mysteries © 2010 by Bill Doyle, Scholastic Inc.

Foul Play

Trapped in the Net

Before Reading

Background Building

This mystery is set in a basketball arena during halftime. Have students describe what they know about halftimes of big sporting events. What is the point of a halftime show? Who might perform? Are audience members watching at home? Ask if students find these shows entertaining.

Focus of Reading Strategy:
Making Inferences

Remind students that an inference involves combining clues in the text with one's own experiences to draw conclusions and make judgments. In this story, the crook never admits to any wrongdoing. Ask students to infer what his motives might be.

After Reading

Talk About It

Ask students if they think there might be a need for a "sports detective" like T.D. in the real world. What would such a detective do? What kinds of cases would he or she solve? Discuss with students if they would like to be a sports detective.

Write About It

Cut out movie, book, or restaurant reviews from the newspaper to share with the class. Point out that a reviewer is someone who offers a description and an opinion (including criticism and praise) of different events or works of art. Ask students to pretend they are reviewers for the local newspaper. Have them write a review of the halftime show in this story.

Vocabulary

Here's a list of words your students will come across in this mystery—as well as their definitions:

aliens	beings from another planet
attracted	drawn to
aviators	pilots; in this case, Aviators is the name of a team
bandits	enemy aircraft; in this case, Bandits is another team name
chaos	state of confusion and disorder
countered	argued back
magnetic	able to attract
personality	noticeable traits that distinguish a person
repel	push away
sabotaged	destroyed in order to undermine someone's achievements
skittered	moved with quick, scampering steps
strewn	scattered about
unconvincing	unbelievable
unnecessary	not needed
urgently	showing a wish for something to be done quickly

Trapped in the Net

When mystery transforms a halftime show into a hilarious mess, T.D. takes to the basketball court to crack the case.

"Ladies and gentlemen!" the announcer's voice boomed over the basketball arena's loudspeakers. "Please give a great, big welcome to our halftime show performers!"

Up in the stands, T.D. brought his hands together lazily once or twice. His dad, who sat next to him, nudged him in the ribs. "Come on, T.D.," Mr. Davies said with a chuckle. "You can show a little more enthusiasm than that."

"All right, Dad." T.D. clapped twice more, but that was it. There were two reasons he couldn't get more excited.

Comprehension Cliffhangers: Mysteries © 2010 by Bill Doyle, Scholastic Inc.

For one thing, the 12-year-old sports detective was not a fan of halftime shows. The performances could be really silly sometimes and just plain goofy the rest of time. And T.D. felt sure that the one about to start on the court of Hunter Basketball Arena wasn't going to be an exception.

But the real reason he didn't feel like clapping was because of the first half of the basketball game. His favorite team, the Bandits, was losing to the Aviators by 42 points. This was thanks mostly to the Aviators' point guard, Gary Garrison. The guy was not only a whiz at science—his hobby was working with magnets—Garrison was also a whiz on the court. He couldn't miss a shot tonight. He got every rebound. And he caught every pass.

Even the coin toss at the beginning of the game had gone Garrison's way. Literally. Instead of starting the game with a jump ball, the basketball league flips a special "game coin" to see which team would get the ball. When the referee tossed the metal coin, it spun toward Garrison.

While Garrison was playing his best, the Bandits had never played worse. None of the Bandits' shots went through the hoop—the ball either bounced off the rim or missed it altogether. The only time the Bandits had scored was when players slam-dunked the ball.

T.D. was frustrated by all of this—and so were the Bandits. In fact, one of them had shoved Garrison too hard while going up for a rebound, sending him tumbling to the ground. But Garrison had popped back up. And before leaving the court at halftime, he had jumped and touched both hoops, probably to show the Bandits they couldn't keep him down.

"WAAAAAHHHHHHH!"

This screech snapped T.D. out of his thoughts of the dismal first half. The sound was coming from the court, where the halftime show was under way. One of the performers was dressed in a space alien costume with three-foot-long metal antennae. He was driving a tinfoil-covered golf cart around in circles on one half of the court. Each time the cart got close to one of the other performers dressed like aliens, they would all scream "WAAAAAHHHHH!" for some reason. It was really annoying, and T.D. guessed it was part of the performance.

On the other side of the court, a man was dressed up like a knight. He was riding one of those fake horses with a metal head at the top and a broomstick for a body. The knight was prancing around on the phony pony and pretending to do battle with a papier-mâché dragon.

T.D. groaned. There wasn't just one halftime show. Instead, there were two shows going on at once on either side of the court. That meant two times the silliness.

"What does any of this have to do with basketball?" T.D. complained.

"It's a halftime contest," his dad explained. "Two groups are putting on shows with Hollywood themes. One group is doing science fiction, and the other is doing adventure films. At the end of halftime, the audience will cheer.

Whichever group gets the loudest applause will win. Get it?"

"Yeah, I got it," T.D. moaned. "Like a bad cold." Science fiction and adventure? Why couldn't they do something cool, like a detective theme? Something with a little mystery?

But then, as T.D. watched, things started to get a little interesting.

The alien was still driving the cart in circles, but they were getting a little wider. Each time the alien passed by the basketball hoop, his long metal antennae seemed to bend toward it. On one last turn, the antennae bent so far over that the alien was dragged partway out of the golf cart. The top of his body hit the court floor with a smack, but his legs were still inside the cart—and the cart was still moving!

"Whoa!" T.D. cried, and he wasn't alone. This new development had caught the rest of the audience's attention, and there were shouts of alarm and a few bursts of laughter.

The cart bumped its way over to the land of adventure, with the alien being dragged along and shouting, "WAAAAAHHHHH!" This time, however, the cry wasn't part of the performance.

Hearing the shouting, the knight spun around just as the golf cart rammed into him, sending his metal horse flying across the court. T.D. watched as the horse skittered into the science fiction area, stopped, and then kept moving toward the hoop very slowly, as if on its own.

Finally, the golf cart collided with the fake dragon and flipped over. It came to a halt upside down, with its wheels still spinning in the air.

The audience went nuts, cheering and clapping and shouting.

But not T.D. He was busy watching the fake horse still moving on its own toward the basketball hoop.

That's when T.D. realized there was mystery in the halftime show after all. "We better get down there, Dad," he said urgently. "We have to talk to the refs, and fast!"

His dad chuckled again. "The halftime show was bad, but the referees can't do anything. What do you want them to do, call 'unnecessary silliness?'"

Ignoring the joke, T.D. took off running and called over his shoulder, "Come on, Dad!"

When T.D. and his dad got down on the court, the performers from the competing shows were arguing with each other. The alien had removed his mask, and he was yelling at the knight. "I don't know how you did it, but you sabotaged our show!"

The knight yelled back, "I wasn't the one who drove a stupid tinfoil car through your performance!"

"Shows what you know," the alien countered. "It's not a tinfoil car. It's a Martian rover."

"Hey!" Mr. Davies stepped between them, attempting to keep them apart. Meanwhile, T.D. was trying to figure out what could have caused the accident.

Just then, the coaches and the players were returning from the locker rooms to warm up before the start of the second half. When they spotted the chaos, the Bandits and the Aviators players frowned. The court was strewn with pieces of the papier-mâché dragon, the upside-down rover, scattered Martian rocks, the fake horse, and angry performers. It was a disaster area.

Coach Williams of the Bandits was standing close to T.D. "These performers are having as much luck as my players," the coach said. "I can't make heads or tails of what's going on."

This last phrase helped T.D. put everything together. "Of course!" T.D. exclaimed. "Coach, I know who messed up this halftime show. And I know why your team is losing like crazy to the Aviators!"

"What?" Coach Williams and T.D.'s dad asked at the same time. Even the alien and the knight stopped fighting long enough to stare at him.

Smiling, T.D. walked over to the referee. "Normally, I might charge a little more to solve the mystery," he said. "But today, all I need is one coin."

Discussion Questions

1. What kind of event is taking place during halftime at the basketball game? Is there a competition? Why doesn't T.D. like halftime shows?

2. Why isn't T.D. happy with how his favorite team, the Bandits, is playing? Is there a player on the other team, the Aviators, who really stands out? Why?

3. What happens to the alien who is driving the golf cart? Why does the alien think the knight sabotaged his performance?

4. In the first part of the story, the word *metal* is used to describe different items. Do you think that's important? Why? Does it have something to do with the coin T.D. requests?

OKAY! **Now keep reading to see if you solved the mystery!**

With a shrug, the referee handed T.D. the metal coin used in the coin toss.

"Thanks," he said. With his dad, the coaches, the players, and even the audience watching him, T.D. walked toward the hoop on the side of the court where the alien had fallen off the cart. T.D. tossed the coin in the air. It spun and then curved toward the hoop, finally landing on it with a clang.

There were a few gasps of surprise. "How did you do that?" the alien said.

"You crashed your cart because you lost control, right?" T.D. asked.

"That's right," the alien answered. "It felt like something was pulling on my antennae. I thought I must be imagining it."

"Something *was* yanking your antennae." T.D. turned his gaze on the Aviators team, and his eyes went straight to Gary Garrison. The point guard was trying to take off his wristbands.

"Stop him!" T.D. shouted. "He's a cheater, and he's trying to hide the evidence!"

This got the full attention of the referee. "What's going on?" he demanded. "Who's cheating?"

T.D. pointed at Gary Garrison. "He put magnets around one hoop and inside the ball so that his shots would be attracted to the hoop. He put another magnet in the other hoop to repel the ball every time the Bandits took a shot."

"That's why my players only scored when they went for slam dunks!" the coach of the Bandits said excitedly.

"When he left the court," T.D. continued, "Garrison tapped the rims of both hoops. I think he was switching the magnets because he knew he'd be shooting into the other hoop in the second half. Plus, magnets in his wristbands made sure he always caught the ball. That's why the coin used in the original coin toss curved toward him."

Now all eyes had turned to Garrison. He had put his hands behind his back, trying to hide his wristbands.

"I'm innocent. Magnets are just my hobby!" Gary Garrison cried, sounding really unconvincing. "Can I help it if the ball always comes to me? Maybe I just have a magnetic personality!"

Rolling his eyes, T.D. said, "Leave the bad acting for the halftime show, Garrison!"

The audience heard this and started laughing. And they kept cheering as two referees led Gary Garrison off the court.

"Looks like we have a winner of the halftime competition!" the announcer shouted over the loudspeaker as a spotlight swung over to T.D.

His dad leaned over and asked T.D., "What do you think of halftime shows now?"

With the spotlight on him and all the applause coming his way, T.D. didn't think they were so silly anymore.

Comprehension Cliffhangers: Mysteries © 2010 by Bill Doyle, Scholastic Inc.